D1498123

Land Markets and
Land Policy in a
Metropolitan Area

Books from the Lincoln Institute of Land Policy/OG&H

Land Acquisition in Developing Countries
Michael G. Kitay

Introduction to Computer Assisted Valuation
Edited by Arlo Woolery and Sharon Shea

Second World Congress on Land Policy, 1983
Edited by Matthew Cullen and Sharon Woolery

The Zoning Game Revisited
Richard F. Babcock and Charles L. Siemon

Advanced Industrial Development
Donald Hicks

Land Supply Monitoring
David R. Godschalk, Scott A. Bollens, John S. Hekman,
and Mike E. Miles

The Urban Caldron
Edited by Joseph DiMento, LeRoy Graymer, and Frank Schnidman

Land Readjustment: The Japanese System
Luciano Minerbi, Peter Nakamura, Kiyoko Nitz, and Jane Yanai

Measuring Fiscal Capacity
Edited by H. Clyde Reeves

Economics and Tax Policy
Karl E. Case

A Redefinition of Real Estate Appraisal Precepts and Processes
Edited by William N. Kinnard, Jr.

Land Markets and Land Policy in a Metropolitan Area

A Case Study of Tokyo

Yuzuru Hanayama

A Lincoln Institute of Land Policy Book

Published by
Oelgeschlager, Gunn & Hain
in association with the
Lincoln Institute of Land Policy

International Standard Book Number: 0-89946-197-2

Library of Congress Catalog Card Number: 85-13867

Printed in the U.S.A.

Oelgeschlager, Gunn & Hain, Publishers, Inc.
131 Clarendon Street
Boston, MA 02116

Library of Congress Cataloging in Publication Data

Hanayama, Yuzuru, 1939-
    Land markets and land policy in a metropolitan area.

    "A Lincoln Institute of Land Policy book."
    Includes index.
    1. Land use, Urban—Government policy—Japan—Tokyo Metropolitan Area. 2. Real property—Prices—Japan—Tokyo Metropolitan Area. 3. Real estate development—Japan—Tokyo Metropolitan Area. I. Title.
HD920.T62H36 1985   333.77′13′0952135   85-13867
ISBN 0-89946-197-2

Contents

List of Figures

List of Tables

Lincoln Institute Foreword

The Lincoln Institute of Land Policy is an educational institute dedicated to the development and exchange of ideas and information pertaining to land policy and property taxation. It is a school offering opportunities for instruction and research. It welcomes government officials, working practitioners, and students to the pursuit of advanced studies.

The Lincoln Institute is also a center for linking the university and the practice of government; for bringing together scholars, professionals, and officials; and for blending the theory and practice of land policy.

We have the opportunity to work with many academics and practitioners during our research and program activity. In June 1980, Professor Hanayama and Mr. Tokunosuke Hasegawa of the Japan Housing Corporation presented a paper at the World Congress on Land Policy in Cambridge, Massachusetts. That paper, "The Land-Market Structure on the Fringe of Tokyo," served as a basic concept piece for this book. During the period of the expansion of the paper to this book, the Lincoln Institute is grateful for the assistance of Harvard Graduate School of Design Professor William A. Doebele.

International case studies of land markets are rare, and we are pleased to be able to publish this work. We hope this book will assist policymakers and practitioners in their tasks of setting land policy and implementing land use regulatory programs.

Frank Schnidman
Senior Fellow
December 1985

Preface

In spite of great economic growth during the past few decades, housing conditions for the Japanese people, particularly for the working class in major metropolitan areas, have not improved—in fact, they have worsened. It is not a coincidence that Tokyo, the capital of Japan, displays both affluence in industrial products and lack of effective land use planning. Its many skyscrapers, rising one after another above the horizon, are juxtaposed with old, tiny wooden apartment houses just outside the downtown areas.

The most important reason for the poor condition of housing in Tokyo is a rapid rise in land prices. As a matter of fact, land prices in residential areas in the suburbs of Tokyo increased twenty times during the 1960–1980 period, while real national income per capita approximately quadrupled and the consumer price index trebled.

One can easily point out the deleterious effects of this rapid increase in prices for housing land:

1. It prevents local governments from providing adequate urban infrastructure, including such facilities as roads, water supply and sewage pipelines, and parks and schools.
2. Landowners tend to resist any land use control that may deprive them of the value of their properties.
3. It brings forth a retrogressive income distribution. More specifically, it widens the income discrepancy between the households that have land to sell or let and those that have to buy or rent land.

To cope with these problems, it would be advisable to curb land price inflation. The Japanese people, however, seem to have despaired of any political remedy. Their distrust of land policy involves a myth that land policy is completely futile. This myth of the futility, along with the myth of the land shortage and the myth of the continuous rise in land prices, has made land a fetish with supernatural power to bring happiness to those who possess it. At the present people struggle with each other to get land when they should cooperate in coping with the problems by studying the actual cause of their land and housing difficulties.

This book consists of six chapters. In Chapter 1 three myths are described and analyzed. Chapter 2 provides thumbnail sketches of the historical evolution of the Tokyo metropolitan area and development of land policy. Chapter 3 is devoted to analysis of Tokyo-area land markets in 1960s and 1970s; this is one of the results of an empirical survey that I have done to study the structure of the land market. In Chapters 4 and 5, several policy instruments are examined from a pragmatic point of view. Finally, Chapter 6 presents a proposal for an integration of policy instruments to solve Tokyo's land problems. It is crucial that we understand that at least one effective and viable land policy exists so that we can abandon our current myths and recover the spirit to challenge the problem.

This book is written on the basis of Japanese data, particularly for Tokyo. I believe, though, that the Japanese experience contains lessons for other countries because it shows both the bright and the dark sides of economic growth that many other countries are trying to pursue with an eye to the bright side only.

Yuzuru Hanayama

Acknowledgments

In writing this book I have acquired many debts. Some of these I should like to acknowledge here. I am much obliged to Professor William A. Doebele of Harvard University, who read the manuscript repeatedly and gave me a great deal of invaluable advice.

Both Thomas T. Tompson and Gil Latz, the first foreign readers of the manuscript, offered many ideas for improvement, and Hirokatsu Ogasawara helped with English usage and expression.

I am also greatly indebted to Professor Kagato Shinzawa, who was my adviser when I was a graduate student at the University of Tokyo. He read the Japanese manuscript carefully and gave me many helpful comments.

Finally, I would like to thank Akiko Iwai, Hiroya Ono, Tomohiko Ikeno, and Toshiki Hiramatsu for helping me with typing and the creation of tables and figures.

1

Three Myths About Housing Land

The Japanese people believe three myths about housing land: the myth of the housing land shortage, the myth of continuous increases in land prices, and the myth of the futility of land policies. These myths have so preoccupied the Japanese mind that land seems to have developed a supernatural power to bring happiness to the people who possess it. It is necessary to analyze these myths before analyzing the land problems that plague Japan today.

Section 1. The Myth of the Housing Land Shortage

Kakuei Tanaka's Calculation

Japanese land price increases have been most notable in metropolitan areas, especially in the Tokyo Region. These increases often have been attributed to the concentration of population into Tokyo's limited land space. For instance, the "General Principles of Urban Policy (Interim Report)," which the Urban Policy Research Council of the Liberal-Democratic Party (LDP) announced in 1968, included the following:

> The 27 million population in the Tokyo region as of 1965 is expected to reach 37 million in 1985. If each household should be provided with its residential house on a 50-tsubo plot, the population would need a total of urbanized space as large as 3,900 sq km, including public spaces, thus exceeding 60 percent of the acreage of all lowlands in the Kanto District.

(Note: The tsubo is the traditional housing plot measuring standard in Japan and equals 6 x 6 ft; in other words, 50 tsubo = 1,800 sq ft = 165 sq m or approximately one-twenty-fifth of an acre.)

Kakuei Tanaka, prime minister from 1972 to 1974, who is said to have played an important role in the compilation of these general principles, further elaborates on the above description in his bestselling book *Building a New Japan* (Nikkan Kogyo Shinbun 1972:33):

> If you place the compass needle at the center of Tokyo (the Zero Milestone at Nihonbashi) and swing a circle with a radius of 50 kilometers, this circle will range over such cities as Chigasaki in Kanagawa Prefecture and Ryugasaki in Ibaraki Prefecture. If you do the same for Osaka and Nagoya with the JNR (Japan National Railways Corporation) Osaka and Nagoya Stations, respectively, as their centers, the Osaka circle will encompass Akashi in Hyogo Prefecture and Otsu in Shiga Prefecture, while the Nagoya circle would include Sekigahara in Gifu Prefecture and Gamagoori in Aichi Prefecture.
>
> According to the 1970 National Census, 33 million people live within 50 kilometers from the centers of Japan's three largest cities. This means that 32 percent of the total population lives on 1 percent of total land acreage. Japan has a total area smaller than the single State of California and a population as large as Spain's on less than 1 percent of its land. One may well wonder if such a state is said to cause no problems at all.

Both the "General Principles" and *Building a New Japan* attracted sensational public attention on publication and had significant influence on urban policy. However, they were based on a belief that the land price increases and the housing difficulties in large cities were the inevitable outcomes of the relative shortage of land as compared to large urban populations. From this belief Tanaka derived a policy that would deconcentrate population into rural areas plus provide a massive supply of high-rise condominium housing buildings for urban redevelopment. These activities reinforced a typical myth about land—that is, "land is scarce."

This myth is not supported by an analysis of the available figures. In the Third Comprehensive National Land Development Program (1977), the population of the Tokyo Region is estimated for 1985 at 31.2 million persons. The New Comprehensive National Land Development Program (1969) provided for an entire National Capital Sphere population of 40.5 million persons, of which the urban area population in the Tokyo Region is estimated at 25 million. Therefore, the 37 million figure referred to in the "General Principles of Urban Policy" is exaggerated.

Let us further examine the figures cited in *Building a New Japan*. The land acreage of the Tokyo, Osaka, and Nagoya within 50 km from the city centers are, respectively, 7,609 sq km, 7,349 sq km, and 7,308 sq km, totaling 22,266 sq km, or 5.9 percent of the total land space of Japan, which is 377,535 sq km. In other words, the acreage of those three cities is a great deal more than 1 percent of the total land space of Japan that Tanaka claims. On the other hand, with respect to the population, those in the three areas are, respectively, 21,950,000, 13,640,000, and 6,770,000 persons, totaling 42,360,000 persons and accounting for 40.8 percent of the total population of Japan—not the claimed 32 percent. The figures cited by Tanaka are remarkably inaccurate, and he cited such figures to give readers an exaggerated impression of land shortages in major urban areas. A description such as "32 percent of the national population live in 1 percent of the total land space" leads one to conclude that the area is heavily overpopulated. These figures, however, are unfounded. For instance, with a total of the land acreage of the three areas divided by the population therein (within 50 km from the city centers), the per capita land space is 526 sq m, thus providing 1,577 sq m of land space for a standard household of three persons. If 60 percent of the land space is allocated for public, commercial, and other business spaces (see Table 1.2.), there still would be enough for 630 sq m of housing plot per household, which is much larger than said 50 tsubo.

Most deceptive is the reference to 3,900 sq km as "exceeding 60 percent of the acreage of all lowlands in the Kanto District." This description suggests that more than half of the Kanto Plain has been turned into housing plots, which has not yet occurred.

On a map the Kanto Plain is nearly rectangular, about 130 km from the east to the west and 100 km from the north to the south, thus making a total acreage of approximately 13,000 sq km. Even if 3,900 sq km are urbanized, that is only one-third of the acreage of the Kanto Plain. The deception is made even trickier by the use of such vague terms as the *lowlands* in the Kanto District, which do not have an acceptable definition. Provided that the lowlands can be defined as the alluviums, the total acreage of alluvial surfaces in Tokyo and surrounding prefectures (Chiba, Saitama, Kanagawa, Ibaraki, Tochigi, and Gunma Prefectures) is about 5,500 sq km, and the 3,900 sq km certainly equals about 70 percent of it. However, there is no reason for locating town areas only on the alluvial formations. The residential quarters in Tokyo are sited on the diluvial formations, as is discernible from the fact that these as a whole are generally referred to as yamanote (highland area), including the town of Mejiro (where Tanaka's residence is located). Such subcenters of Tokyo as Shinjuku and Ikebukuro are also on the heights. All the diluvial formation in the Kanto Plain is flat and has good conditions for urban development. According to the National Geographical Survey (1975), the total area of the Kanto Plain, including both alluvial and diluvial formations, is 15,231 sq km: 3,900 sq km is only 26 percent of it.

Land Is Not Short

The acreage of the Tokyo Region within 50 km from its center is 7,609 sq km, inhabited by 21,950,000 persons, according to the 1970 census, thus providing 347 sq m of land space per person. This space is notably small as compared to the average of the three major urban areas. Yet, with a share of housing land space in an urban area presumed at 40 percent of its total acreage, the average housing land space per household in the Tokyo Region would reach 410 sq m.

Some people may claim that an area ranging from 50 km from the city center is too large to be a standard for a discussion of housing land problems. It is true that within a radius of 50 km are places inadequate for housing because of the scarcity of commuter transportation leading to the business centers. Good farm land spaces in the area should preferably be excluded from urbanization. It is by no means easy to identify the land spaces for urban housing and those qualified for nonurbanization. When the City Planning Law was substantially amended in 1978, it created an urbanization promotion area (UPA), which was "the area which has already been urbanized and those which will be urbanized within 10 years on the preferential and planned basis." In this respect, the urbanization zones in Tokyo and the adjacent prefectures (Chiba, Saitama, and Kanagawa Prefectures as shown in Figure 1.1.) can be determined to be the urban area in the Tokyo Region.

The UPA was designated in 1970. As Table 1.1. shows, the total acreage of the UPA in Tokyo and the three prefectures was 3,162 sq km. The population therein is 20,760,000, and the per capita land space is 152 sq m, which leads to a housing space per household of 182 sq m. Certainly this is not large enough for a household, but it is still more space than the 50 tsubo that is claimed as a housing standard by Tanaka.

Behind the housing land difficulty lies a shortage of housing land not in terms of absolute space but rather in terms of distribution. For instance, according to the 1979 edition of the Tokyo metropolitan government's annual report, "The Land in Tokyo," the total of privately owned land in the twenty-three wards (the old metropolitan area, which is under the UPA) is 25,885 hectares held by 826,015 individuals. The average of privately owned land space is 313 sq m per owner. However, those who own 10,000 sq m or more of land per person share 14.5 percent of 25,885 hectares, despite the fact that they comprise only 3 percent of all private landowners or 0.3 percent of the total population therein. On the other hand, the minor landowners who hold 100 sq m or less of land per person equal 42.9 percent of the total population, though their share of land is 8.4 percent. What is more, the miniland-owners who hold 50 sq m or less of land each total 13.6 percent of all

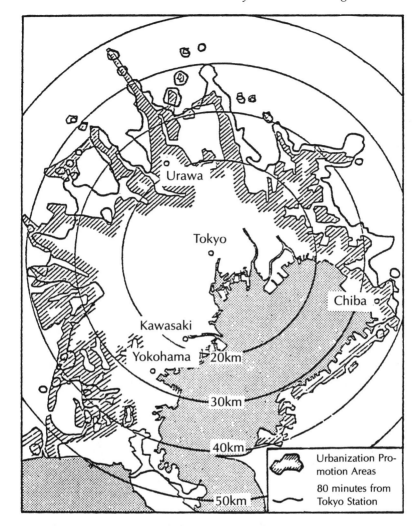

Figure 1.1. *Urbanization promotion areas in the Tokyo region.*

landowners, but their share of land is limited to 1.5 percent. If the number of nonlanded households in the twenty-three wards were included, the inequality in land distribution would become more obvious.

Among the large landowners are those who own large housing land units, although most own farmland and wooded land. In other words, the UPAs in the middle part of Tokyo are interwoven with many farmlands and wooded lands, which explains why the earlier calculated housing land space per household was larger than one might have thought:

Table 1.1.
Urban Land Areas in the Tokyo Region (1970)

	City planning area		Urbanization promotion areas		Densely inhabited districts	
	A	P	A	P	A	P
Tokyo	162,916	11,378	104,124	11,307	80,560	10,874
Chiba	261,365	2,819	60,111	1,783	22,926	1,700
Saitama	262,056	3,735	63,875	2,732	26,820	2,126
Kanagawa	192,571	5,455	88,049	4,934	50,250	4,290
Total	878,908	23,387	316,159	20,756	180,556	18,990

Note: A = Area in hectares (1 ha = 10,000 sq m)
P = Population (1000 persons).
Source: Ministry of Construction, *Takuchi Yōran* (Housing Land Handbook) 1977.

It has been calculated with the farmland and wooded land also included as available housing land.

Table 1.2. shows a breakdown by use of land in the UPA in Tokyo and the three adjacent prefectures. As of 1978 about 60,000 hectares of farmland and 20,000 hectares of wooded land were included in the UPA in these prefectures: In other words, about one-quarter of the UPAs are used as either farmland or wooded land. Of course, these farmlands and wooded lands are not extensive compared with the entire land of Japan. For instance, the proportion of these lands in Tokyo and the three prefectures are, respectively, one-hundredth and one-thousandth of all the farmlands and wooded lands in Japan. Still, if these could be made convertible into housing land, their contribution to easing the housing land difficulty in the area would be immeasurable.

According to the Construction Ministry's "Survey of Actual Housing Demand" in 1978, the number of "housing needy" households, which includes either "in difficulty" or "in extreme difficulty," totaled 2,760,000 households in the Tokyo Region, or 38.6 percent of all ordinary households in the region. If the 83,150 hectares of farmlands and wooded lands in the UPA therein could all be distributed equally to these "housing needy" households, each household would receive 301 sq m of housing plot. Even with 60 percent of the distributable land reserved for public, commercial, and industrial uses, each household would still be entitled to 120 sq m, which is equivalent to the net housing land space per household of the Tama New Town Project, which is the largest and best quality housing project in the Tokyo Metropolitan Area.

The expected effect of the above-assumed conversion of farm and wooded lands into housing land has also been ascertained by aerial photography. According to the Japan Housing Corporation's analysis

Table 1.2.
Land Use in the UPA in the Tokyo Region
(*hectare*)

Category	Tokyo	Chiba	Saitama	Kanagawa	Total	Proportion of total land (%)	Proportion of developed land (%) [1]
Built-up Land	66,252	28,764	27,626	50,019	172,661	54.6	83.8
Residential	37,239	15,138	16,333	29,434	98,144	(31.1)	(47.6)
Commercial	3,584	1,073	1,072	1,586	7,315	(2.3)	(3.6)
Industrial	12,929	9,256	5,704	12,046	39,935	(12.6)	(19.4)
Public	12,500	3,297	4,517	6,953	27,267	(8.6)	(13.2)
Road	10,747	5,464	5,368	6,792	28,371	9.0	13.8
Park	2,578	467	496	1,484	5,025	1.6	2.4
River	1,867	176	1,057	1,419	4,519	1.4	–
Farmland	9,921	11,923	24,089	14,099	60,032	19.0	–
Woodland	2,309	7,368	3,480	9,961	23,118	7.3	–
Miscellaneous	10,450	5,949	1,759	4,275	22,433	7.1	–
Total	104,123	60,111	63,875	88,049	316,159	100.0	100.0

[1]Total of built-up land, road, and park.

of aerial photographs of Tokyo and the three prefectures, there were 2,612 open spaces (*open space* herein defined as a space of three hectares or more of vacant land) in the UPA in Tokyo and the three prefectures but one or more hectares of space in the twenty-three wards in Tokyo and the three central wards in Yokohama), thus totaling 38,945 hectares (see Table 1.3.). In the case of medium-rise condominium buildings to be constructed by the Japan Housing Corporation, the household density (the ratio of households to land space) is around 100 households per hectare (population density is around 300 persons) with nearly 40 percent of land space reserved for public spaces. Therefore, if all the available spaces are developed for housing projects, the corporation would be able to provide apartments for about 2.6 million or more households. Unlike the subjective concept of "housing needy" household that was used in the "Survey of Actual Housing Requirement," the "Statistical Survey on Housing" published by the prime minister's office in 1978 used some objective standards to estimate the number of "housing-poor" households. Its minimum standard of a household requires a bedroom for the parents, a separate bedroom for each dependent age 18 or older, and separate bedrooms for boys and girls between ages 6 and 17 years (however, with not more than two beds per bedroom). The size of the bedroom for the parents is six tatami (3 x 6 feet) mats or larger, the bedroom for children is 4.5 tatami mats or larger, and the dining room-kitchen is 4.5 tatami mats or larger for a family with four members or less, but six mats or larger for a family with five members or more). By this standard, there are more than 1,290,000

Table 1.3.
Vacant Lots in the UPA in the Tokyo Region

	All		<10 ha		10–30 ha		30–50 ha		>50 ha	
	No	ha	No	ha	No	ha	No	ha	No	ha
Tokyo	515	5,410	377	1,608	102	1,688	22	834	14	1,280
Chiba	612	12,818	327	2,005	177	3,035	65	2,390	43	5,388
Saitama	866	12,031	520	2,943	255	4,037	51	1,939	40	3,112
Kanagawa	628	8,686	409	2,319	161	2,546	31	1,139	27	2,682
Total	2,621	38,945	1,633	8,875	695	11,306	169	6,302	124	12,462

Source: Tokunosuke Hasegawa, "Shutoken Kinkō Seibi Chitai ni Okeru Kūkanchi no Fuzon Jōkyō" (Distribution of Vacant Lots in Suburbs of the National Capitol Region), *Takuchi Kaihatsu* (Housing Land Development), No. 60 (1978).

housing-poor households living in substandard rental houses or apartments in the Tokyo Region, thus comprising 15.5 percent of all the ordinary households. If the Japan Housing Corporation were able to act for the construction of housing buildings as earlier calculated, the housing difficulty in the region would immediately be solved.

The Tokyo Region is notorious for its housing problems, but even in this region the main cause of the difficulty is not a land shortage. It is true that not all of the vacant land spaces in the UPA are readily available for housing construction. Environmental arrangements for public transportation, city water and sewage service systems, and school facilities are needed. Moreover, the abnormal influx of population into the Tokyo Region demonstrates that strenuous efforts would be needed to manage the overpopulation in this region. There should be a clear difference between an urban policy package arising from a recognition that land is short and one derived from a recognition that land is not short at all. Both the "General Principles of Urban Policy" and *Building a New Japan* intentionally misled people to believe in a land shortage, which limited the range of land policy options.

When the required per person acreage of housing land and its potential supply are taken into account, land is not short in the Tokyo Region. To believe in the myth of land shortage is tantamount to admitting to the impossibility of increasing the liquidity of land. The myth of land shortage represents a conservativism that resists changing trends already established.

Section 2. The Myth of the Continuous Increase in Land Prices

The National Land Agency's Explanation of Land Price Rise

One of the most significant legacies from the high economic growth period was the myth that land prices will inevitably continue to rise. Because of this myth, people who needed housing land borrowed money to buy land while its prices were still within their reach, and even entrepreneurs not in the real estate trade tried to buy land as extensively as was permissible. This myth also led landowners to believe that they can expect more economic advantages from holding land than selling it. They thought that as long as they possessed land, its worth would annually increase at a rate as high as 20 percent, while the gain that they could expect from financial assets such as corporate debentures—which they might purchase with an income from land sales—would be at best only around 10 percent per annum. Consequently, the land price rises were accelerated, with demand on the land market having rapidly expanded against slow supply. A land price rise at one place touched off more price rises at the others, thus still more deeply rooting belief in this myth. Even after the slowdown of economic growth in Japan following the first oil crises, which led to a significant recession in the demand for land, the myth has persisted.

Land prices have continued rising; this fact is undeniable. However, while science determines the law or mechanism lying behind fact, myth misleads people into a belief that what occurred in the past will infallibly recur in the future. The earlier quoted *Building a New Japan* and the "General Principles of Urban Policy" described the general trend of land price rises in the past, but neither of them adequately analyzed its causes.

In 1975 the National Land Agency published the first "White Paper on National Land Utilization," which can be said to have announced the government's official view on land price rises. The White Paper (1979:89) wrote as follows:

> The land price in post-war Japan rose together with the growth of her economy.
>
> From 1955 to 1965, Japanese GNP increased by 15 times from around Yen 9 trillion to around Yen 132 trillion, and the urban land prices throughout the country also rose as high as 28 times.
>
> It can be said in the long-term aspect that along with the accumulation of capital stock and the qualitative improvement of labor in the process of economic growth, the productivity of land rises, thereby leveling the land

price upward. The annual value rise rate for land in its upward movement varied nearly in parallel with the variance of the annual economic growth rate. The land price rises after 1955 were particularly notable from 1956 to 1957, from 1960 to 1961, from 1967 to 1969 and from 1972 to 1973, thus corresponding to the business boom or upward movement periods of the Japanese economy.

The White Paper also included what is shown as Figure 1.2. in this book. The vertical scale indicates the percentage rise of land price and GNP over the previous year, which misleads the reader who understands that land actually increases in value along with the annual economic growth rate (White Paper 1979:89).

> The expansion of business activities accelerates the rise of land price because it leads to more demand for land in various categories. More demand for industrial and commercial use land units based on corporate investment in plants and equipment, demand expansion for public land in the case where a business boom leads to expansion of public spendings, demand growth for housing land owing to increased investment in the private housing sector, and demand expansion for land as a target for investment in the case where the expansion of business activities causes the easing of money market; these are conceivably the factors which cause the land price to rise higher."

Though the White Paper thereafter deals with the relationship between economic growth and by-category demand for land, it deals exclusively with the aspect of demand as the cause of land price rises: In other words, it attributes demand to economic growth.

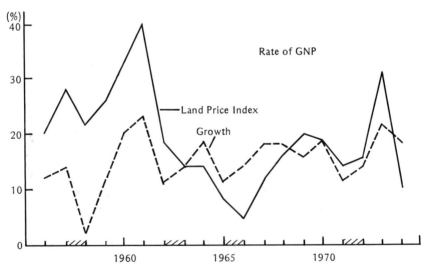

Figure 1.2. *Growth rates of GNP and land price.*

The National Land Agency should have shown Figure 1.3. in the White Paper instead of Figure 1.2. and elaborated on why the land prices alone rose rapidly apart from the upward trend of the wholesale and retail price indexes in the high-growth period of the Japanese economy. The writers of the White Paper then would have had to give thought not only to the demand side but also to the special features of land as a commodity in the supply aspect. The White Paper (1979:89) certainly touches on the supply side, but references to it were limited only to the following comments:

> Land can never be created except for the development of land by reclamation from water. What is more, since most land is actually subject to actual use in one way or another, land supply to meet demand for various categories of land certainly involves the conversion of land use. In cases where such conversion is required in a large scale, it necessitates qualitative changes in terms of land conditions, thus often causing difficulties on the part of the supply side in smoothly responding to demand. Because of the presence of such constraint on the supply side, the rise of land price cannot readily lead to the expansion of quantitative supply.

Although the White Paper points out that the supply of land should logically increase along with the rise of its price but that the quantitative supply lags behind because of the presence of social counterforces, it does not explain how this occurs.

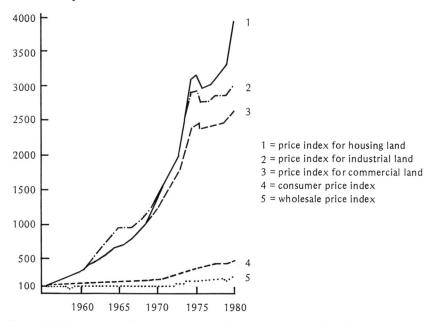

1 = price index for housing land
2 = price index for industrial land
3 = price index for commercial land
4 = consumer price index
5 = wholesale price index

Figure 1.3. *Land price indices in comparison with consumer price indices (1955 = 100).*

Analysis of Actual Land Price Increases

The myth that land prices continue to rise turns into a fetish for land when people apply it to any land and believe that all land prices will continue rising. This fetish misleads people into an illusion that the price of land, wherever it is, will always rise.

It is self-evident to anybody who carefully observes the situation that Japanese land prices did not progress uniformly. Table 1.4. was compiled on the basis of Tokyu Estate Corporation's "Map of Land Price Distribution," in which ten sample sites were selected from each of three groups of housing land estimated at Yen 40,000, Yen 20,000, and Yen 10,000 per sq m, and their price transitions were shown from 1968. Generally speaking, the percentages of increases in land prices in suburban belts were larger than those in the inside areas.

Though the annual land price rises in the suburban belts were most conspicuous in the period from 1970 to 1973, the annual land price rises in the intermediate areas from 1968 to 1970 were more substantial than those in the suburban belts. Moreover, the patterns of land price increases, whether in the suburban belts or in the intermediate areas, were similar to one another, thus suggesting the presence of a regularity, especially in association with the movement of population. In all likelihood the population increases in the intermediate areas had exceeded those in the suburban belts before 1970, the suburban population increases suddenly sped up after 1970, but such population increases as a whole slowed down after 1973.

Table 1.5. seems to corroborate the above assumption for the western part of Tokyo, for instance. The outgoing population spread into the peripheral zones unevenly but shifted from relatively near-town suburban zones to deep suburbs.

In response to this population movement, the tide of housing land

Table 1.4.
Land Price Change

	1968	1970	1973	1976	1970/1968	1973/1970	1976/1973	1976/1968
Outer Core (10-20 km)	40[1]	62	95	125	1.6[2]	1.5	1.3	3.2
Inner Ring (20-30 km)	20	40	72	95	2.0	1.8	1.3	4.8
Outer Ring (30-40 km)	10	17	55	75	1.8	3.1	1.4	7.6

[1]Thousand yen/sq m
[2]Ratio
Note: Land price in this table is the mean value of 10–20 spots.

Table 1.5.
Population Increase in Some Cities in Western Fan-Shaped Sector

Categories	1960	1965	1970	1975	1965/1960	1970/1965	1975/1970	1975/1960
Outer core (six wards)	1,644[1]	1,983	2,161	2,229	1.2[2]	1.1	1.0	1.4
Inner ring (14 cities)	630	1,021	1,340	1,537	1.6	1.3	1.2	2.4
Outer ring (7 cities)	338	484	677	876	1.4	1.4	1.3	2.6

[1]Thousand
[2]Ratio

development also seems to have shifted outward from near-town suburban zones. Figure 1.4. shows this outward shift of housing land development in the near-Tokyo zones, intermediate areas, and deep suburbs in the eastern part of Saitama Prefecture by using the acreage of farmland conversion into housing land as a yardstick. The peak of the converted acreage chronologically moves from Kawaguchi/Soka through Urawa/Koshigaya to Ohmiya/Kasukabe.

However, the outward movement of housing land development does not mean that all the available land units for housing closer to Tokyo have fully been developed. This is obvious from the case of Kawaguchi/Soka in Figure 1.4., which indicates by the dotted line the peak of the converted acreage in 1961 and the second peak in 1976, with the low-level shifting recorded over a long in-between period. What is more, as Table 1.6. compares the farm land acreage in the six cities in Figure 1.4. at the time of the 1970 designation of the urbanization promotion areas (UPA) against those as of the end of 1975, the ratio of the remaining farmland acreage in UPAs to the UPA acreage remains similar to others among these cities.

Thus, the progress of land price rises in the Tokyo Region was not even. It involved notable percentage variances and time lags from one area to another subject to distances from the midtowns in Tokyo, and the peak of such upward price transitions in each area coincided with the time of the major outflow of population from the central part of Tokyo into the area. The peak years came to the near-Tokyo zones before the areas located farther away from Tokyo. However, the geographical shift of housing land demand did not mean that all the available land spaces for housing closer to Tokyo had fully been developed. Therefore, it is difficult to sufficiently explain the causes of land price increases only in terms of demand, and an analysis of the supply-side situation is also needed.

Those who accept the myth of the continuous rise of land prices without empirical analysis thus admit that income redistribution has unfairly been induced by the increases in land prices: The myth implies that the rich will grow richer, while the poor will grow poorer.

Section 3. The Myth of the Futility of Land Policy

Faith in Laissez-Faire

This chapter has noted that both of the myths that land is short and that land prices continue to rise were born out of a conservative mentality and approve a fait accompli. This conservative mentality favors laissez-faire economic activities and rejects land control policy.

Land Policy in this book means a policy that imposes social intervention in one way or another on the private ownership of land. According to the Japanese Civil Code, the ownership of land is "the right to freely use, earn from and/or dispose of land in possession within the statutory

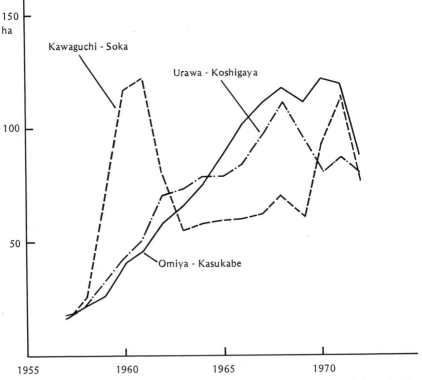

Figure 1.4. *Transfer of farmland to residential plots (moving average of three years).*

Table 1.6.
Decrease of Farm Land in Selected Communities

	UPA	Acreage of farm land (ratio to UPA)				Decrease (rate)	
		1960		*1970*			
Inner Suburbs							
Kawaguchi	4,844 ha	1,904 ha	(39.3%)	1,633 ha	(33.7%)	△271 ha	(△14.2%)
Soka	4,701	2,105	(44.8)	1,654	(35.2)	△451	(△21.4)
Total	9,545	4,009	(42.0)	3,287	(34.4)	△722	(△18.0)
Intermediate Zone							
Urawa	4,390	1,400	(31.9)	1,180	(26.9)	△220	(△15.7)
Koshigaya	2,817	1,356	(48.1)	1,076	(38.2)	△280	(△20.6)
Total	7,207	2,756	(38.2)	2,256	(31.3)	△500	(△18.1)
Deep Suburbs							
Omiya	4,835	1,446	(29.9)	1,203	(24.9)	△243	(△16.8)
Kasukabe	1,848	992	(53.7)	816	(44.2)	△176	(△17.7)
Total	6,683	2,438	(36.5)	2,019	(30.2)	△419	(△17.2)

bounds." Land policy therefore affects three kinds of social interventions: limitation to the exercise of the right to *use* land, taxation on the right to *earn from* land, and expropriation against the right to *dispose of* land. The earlier-quoted *Building a New Japan* proposed industrial relocation and the construction of high-rise apartment buildings in cities but ignored land: It was virtually uninterested in social intervention on the private ownership of land. Its proposals for industrial relocation, "scrap and build" for high-rise apartment buildings, relocation of the capital city, development of green-rich garden cities, and construction of express railroads for commuting deserve serious study. However, these proposals cannot be called a land policy because they do not impose limits on the private ownership of land.

Business organizations such as the Real Estate Trade Associations of Japan more than once have raised objections to social intervention in the private ownership of land and have called for a review or removal of any land use control policies. Their claims for abrogation of the Special Corporate Tax on Capital Gains from Land Transfer also reflect their rejection of restrictive taxation approaches.

What seems to lie beneath this laissez-faire mentality—that is, that land transactions should be left to free competition in the private sector—is a faith in the mechanism of the free market: that the most effective utilization of land is realized through free transfer of land ownership, since a person who can expect the maximum utility of land through its best utilization pays the highest price, while the owner of the land who cannot expect the same utility will prefer to sell it at the proposed price. However, such reliance on the free market crumbles in circumstances where public goods (roads and parks, for example) and externalities (such as suburban access to midtown facilities or a high-rise structure's interference in abuttors' right to enjoy sunshine) play an important role. The free market's functioning for the best utilization of land is unreliable, especially where speculative factors are involved. The myth that land policy does harm to the effective utilization of land can not be logically supported. Even the earlier quoted "General Principles of Urban Policy" included a chapter on land policy that gave preference to the public welfare over private rights with respect to land use.

Basis of the Argument for Land Nationalization

In contrast with the laissez-faire mentality, some arguments claim that there is no better solution to the housing land problem than land nationalization. For instance, Ryotaro Shiba (one of the most popular novelists in Japan) maintains in his article "Land and the Japanese" (1976:209, 217) that "With the germ-contaminated roots of the land problem in Japan deep-spread, there no longer is any other reliable measure but land nationalization to solve it, and I think that 90% of people who live in the Japanese society rally behind this policy as leading in the right direction" and that "Land should be nationalized, just as water and air are in common use." Shiba's allegation that "there no longer is any other reliable measure but land nationalization" implies that because social intervention in the realm of private land ownership is no longer effective, the only recourse is to deny the private ownership of land itself. This position falls at the other end of the spectrum from the laissez-faire approach. If 90 percent of the Japanese really believe that "there is no other recourse but nationalization," then they generally must think that land policy is useless. However, it is not clear that Shiba derived his opinions from a full study of all relevant aspects of land policy.

Such instruments of land policy as land use control, taxation, and expropriation have their intrinsic functions and can be effective within the bounds of those functions. However, there is no panacea for all problems. Shiba's excessive expectations concerning land policy coupled with his lack of familiarity with the specific functions of policy instruments might have led him to distrust land policy as a whole. If the Japanese share his distrust, as he claims, they would also be called on to support still another myth.

Supporting the myth of the futility of land policy—despite the availability of effective land policy—fosters the public's deeply-rooted discontent about land ownership, thus unintentionally or intentionally stimulating a leaning toward totalitarianism. This book challenges the myths about land policy by analyzing their background.

2

Historical Background
and Institutional Settings

For any kind of empirical study, it is important to understand the historical background and institutional framework of the society in question. This chapter is devoted to giving a brief description of these elements in preparation for further analysis in subsequent chapters.

Section 1. Expansion of the Metropolitan Region[1]

Tokyo in the Meiji Era

Previous to his appointment as the eighth governor of Tokyo in 1884, Akimasa Yoshikawa accompanied Hirobumi Itoh to Europe and the United States for an inspection trip and returned with the beginnings of a plan to convert Tokyo into a large modern city. At that time the urban area of Tokyo (which had been called either the Edo Capital Territory or the Red Lined Area during the Edo period) was about 6,000 hectares with a population of 890,000 persons and a population density of 156 persons per hectare. London and Paris, the largest cities in the world at that time, were in size, respectively, about 30,000 hectares (with a city population of 3 million and a population density of 127 persons per hectare) and about 13,000 hectares (with a city population of 2 million and a population density of 157 persons per hectare). Tokyo was much smaller than London and Paris in terms of acreage and population, but its population density was roughly equivalent. Yoshikawa probably considered the possibility of making Tokyo comparable with the two cities by expanding its city area while maintaining the population density at the same level.

The Yoshikawa concept later developed into the Tokyo Municipal Area Reforming Regulational Ordinance (1888), which was the first written law in Japan for city planning, placing the former Capital Territory of the Edo period under the municipality of Tokyo for city planning purposes. However, as capitalism developed in Japan following its industrial revolution, the population influx into Tokyo—the political and economic center of the nation—continued and increased the city population to 1,290,000 as early as 1888 and to about 2,150,000 in 1910 when the City Reforming Plan had nearly been completed. At about the same time population increases became notable in the suburbs adjoining the city area.

There were two types of housing quarters in Tokyo at the end of the last century. One was built for blue-collar workers, and its development coincided with the expanded construction of industrial factories in coastal areas such as Oimachi, Ohsaki-machi, Azuma-machi, and Kameido-machi. The other type of quarters was constructed for white-collar workers and was represented by the housing in Sendagaya-machi, Shibuya-machi, Sugamo-machi, and Nippori-machi. The most heavily populated area at that time, however, was limited to inside the current Yamate Loop Line ring plus both banks of the Sumida River, where the population density exceeded 100 persons per hectare. Outside this area were vast expanses of farm villages where the population density ranged from ten to twenty persons per hectare. In other words, the borders between the municipal area and farm areas were clearly identifiable.

Along with population outflow from the municipal area into suburbs, construction began on suburban private railways such as the Keio Line, Tamagawa Line, Ikegami Electric Trolley Line, Seibu Line, Mekama Electric Trolley Line, and To-Yoko (Tokyo-Yokohama) Electric Trolley Line. In order to secure passengers for these railways, the private railway companies competed with one another to develop housing lands along their own operation belts. The then-farm areas—such as Ebara, Tamagawa, Chofu, Magome, Meguro, Himonya, Ikegami, Setagaya, Matsuzawa, Ochiai, Nogata, and Iogi—were turned into large housing land development sites at the cost of private railway companies.

At the same time, landowners in these farm areas also started developing housing land by making use of the land readjustment approach provided for in the Arable Land Readjustment Law (1899). This law was enacted mainly for the readjustment of inefficient paddyfield pattern and for the elimination of inaccurate rope-based measurements (to correct the officially registered paddyfield acreage in case it was smaller than the actual acreage with a view to increasing rent income from tenancy). Land readjustment is a cooperative activity of landowners who promote the utility of their land by rearranging the boundaries of parcels and constructing roads and other common facilities (see the detailed discussions later in this section and in Chapter 4). Under this approach, landowners were obligated to offer without payment public-use spaces for road construction, but they could expect more earnings than losses due to land price rises. In addition, this law exempted them from the land registration fees when they applied for a package registration of their ownership on newly demarcated plots in exchange for their formerly owned plots.

Tokyo in the Postquake Reconstruction Period

The Great Earthquake of 1923 spurred the sudden population shift from Tokyo into its suburbs as Tokyo citizens moved out of the devastated center into suburbs, and the postquake reconstruction plan scheme (officially, the Imperial Capital City Reconstruction Plan Scheme) also relocated many Tokyo temples, shrines, and factories in the process of its implementation. As a result, the population in such downtown wards as Asakusa, Honjo, and Nihonbashi decreased by 20 to 30 percent, while it doubled and trebled in such suburban towns as Tozuka, Takada, Nishi-Sugamo, and Takinogawa.

The earthquake not only caused a population shift but also affected Tokyo's city structure in a number of important aspects. For instance, a large number of manufacturing facilities in the near midtown areas of Kyobashi, Honjo, and Fukagawa moved to such paddy areas as Kameido and Osaki; and corporate offices and public facilities moved into Marunouchi near the newly built central station of JNR, where the earthquake damage was relatively light, forming a polarization of the city structure. Some subcenters such as Shinjuku, Shibuya, and Ikebukuro surfaced as retail-based commercial centers to accompany the suburbanization of population.

In fact, the earthquake occurred just when Tokyo was ready to start its city planning under the City Planning Law, which had been enacted in 1919 in place of the Tokyo Municipal Area Reforming Regulational Ordinance. The postquake reconstruction, therefore, can be said to have offered a trial arena for the new City Planning Law: The law for the first time provided for zoning and thus introduced the philosophy of designated land uses and land use control.

The city plan after the fire provided for an area covering not only the fifteen wards of Tokyo but also eighty-three towns and villages in its vicinity (a total of 43,000 hectares). The plan thus formed an urban area with a radius of 16 km from the city center and envisioned the formation of the core town area with a population density of 150 persons per hectare surrounded by a suburban belt averaging 75 persons per hectare in density.

Within the plan area were residential quarters to the west (an area described as "high and dry land with its climate and environment pleasant"), the commercial quarters to the east (described as "town streets squarely built with the means of transportation well arranged"), and the industrial quarters adjacent to the Meguro River and Sumida River (flat coastal land described as "already being industrialized with access to navigation").

Immediately after the earthquake, the Special City Planning Law was enacted in December 1923 to make the prescribed arable land readjustment approach in the city also applicable to the quake devastated area in order to facilitate the advancement of the Postquake Reconstruction Scheme. In this connection, Article Eight of the Special City Planning Law provided as follows:

> Within the Reconstruction Enforced Area, in the case where the acreage of a housing land plot after readjustment is confirmed to be over 10 percent smaller than the acreage of the pre-readjustment total of formerly owned land, compensation shall be paid, as set forth in the Imperial Ordinance, for the loss exceeding 10 percent of the initial acreage.

This provision virtually forced all landowners within the reconstruction enforced area to contribute 10 percent of their lands without compensation. Notwithstanding, the contribution ratio was accepted without much resistance under the pressure of the strong power of the imperial government at that time as well as in the name of the reconstruction of the imperial capital city. The Postquake Reconstruction Scheme was completed in seven years, though it involved large-scale rezoning and readjustment ranging over as much as 3,100 hectares (about 70 percent of the devastated acreage), including such midtown wards as Kyobashi, Nihonbash, and Kojimachi. Owing to this scheme, the ratio of public roads in the Rezoning Enforced Area rose to 25 percent from the pre-readjustment 12 percent. Though there were zone differences in the contribution ratio, the average was 15.3 percent, ranging from 5.9 percent at the lowest to 23.1 percent at the highest. It should be kept in mind that nearly one-half of public road acreage in the midtown area of Tokyo consisted of noncompensated lands that had been offered by landowners at the time of the postquake reconstruction.[2]

After the completion of the Postquake Reconstruction Scheme, the city area of Tokyo was expanded in 1932 to the exterior belt roughly along the demarcation line under the prescribed city plan, thus increasing the city area acreage to 47,000 hectares and the population to 5 million (with average population density decreasing to 107 persons from 156 persons per hectare). Compared to Akimasa Yoshikawa's concept, the expanded city of Tokyo was about 7.8 times larger in terms of acreage and 5.6 times larger in terms of population, thus exceeding the size of the city of London at the time. Because the city grew more in acreage than in population, sprawl was already in progress in the suburbs of Tokyo. At the time of the earthquake, Tokyo was planned to accept a population up to 7 million in the city area while keeping population density equivalent to its early years. In other words, the basic position of Tokyo city planning before World War II was to expand the city area in correspondence to its population growth while keeping the population density at a constant level.

The newly expanded city area of Tokyo was in size equivalent to the current twenty-three-ward area of Tokyo metropolis, with 80 percent of it having a population density of 100 persons or near to it per hectare. However, the peripheral areas—such as the current Edogawa, Katsushika, Arakawa, and Nerima wards (which were incorporated in Tokyo city in 1935 and thus are part of the current twenty-three wards—were virtual farm villages with population densities at less than ten persons per hectare.

It should be kept in mind that by 1935, when the suburban housing construction had slowed, only about one-quarter of the population in the city area of Tokyo lived in owner-occupied houses, while three-quarters lived in rental houses. House owners at that time were limited to the wealthy class and traditional town merchants, and most of the residential houses built after the earthquake were rental houses. Among the residential houses built in the suburbs were also many rental houses.

However, beginning around 1943 in the middle of World War II, a large number of industrial facilities and inhabitants either deserted or moved out of the midtown area of Tokyo because the danger of air raids or the imperial government order for evacuation. With 710,000 residential houses—about half the houses in the city area of Tokyo— burnt down, approximately one-third of the city area was destroyed, which was the basic cause of housing shortages in postwar Tokyo. The population of the city of Tokyo also decreased to 2,780,000 persons from its prewar peak of 6,780,000.

Tokyo in the Postwar Reconstruction Period

The Special Urban Planning Law (1946) for the postwar reconstruction of Tokyo, was implemented to rearrange town zoning in the war-devastated areas by using the town plot readjustment approach similar to the one applied to the reconstruction of the quake-devastated areas. The second Special Urban Planning Law was in content virtually the same as the first. The only notable difference between the two laws was the percentage of the compensation-free readjustment loss on the part of landowners: That is, 10 percent under the former and 15 percent under the latter was to be contributed without compensation to public use such as roads and parks. However, the Postwar Reconstruction Plan was ambitious, especially with respect to its road construction arrangements, and the planned readjustment space reduction ratios surpassed 30 percent in most of the affected area. The actual progress of the reconstruction fell far behind schedule due to shortages in the fund for compensable readjustment losses. In addition, landowners showed increasing resistance against the 15 percent standard for noncompensated land contributions. This finally led in 1949 to a revision of the law that provided for compensation "to cover the amount of decrease in the case where the total of postreadjustment values of plots is less than the total of antereadjustment land values."

Finding the funds to finance compensation also raised a big problem at the time of the postquake reconstruction, and the compensation-eligible landowners were paid in public bond certificates instead of cash. It was impossible at the time of the postwar reconstruction to resort to the same financial recourse because of the spiraling price inflation. In addition, with high inflation, it was actually difficult to predict the real worth of expected compensation receivable by landowners for their readjustment losses under the revised law. Therefore, landowners became reluctant to cooperate in the promotion of the War-Devastated Areas Land Readjustment Scheme. The planned readjustment was fully carried out only in 1,110 hectares, 5.6 percent of the 20,000 hectares planned for readjustment under this scheme. More important, the scheme functioned mainly to expand plazas around such railway terminals as Shinjuku, Shibuya, and Gotanda and main traffic arteries in Tokyo, thus leaving largely unachieved the basic purpose of creating well-arranged housing quarters.

The progress of the postwar land readjustment under the Special Urban Planning Law was slow, especially compared to its extensive and ambitious vision of future. Because of the construction of a large number of houses in the rubble of devastated towns, which ran counter to the legally provided housing construction control over the Plan Finalized areas, the Tokyo metropolitan government had to tone down its urban reconstruction plan, even though the original plan had been essential for the ideal implementation of the Special Urban Planning Law.

Revision of the plan was based on the reality that as early as the late 1940s people who evacuated midtown Tokyo in the war years and who were repatriated from overseas colonies after the war started building shabby houses wherever space was available on bomb-torn plots. However, the massive population influx into Tokyo touched off a business boom following the unexpected outbreak of the Korean War, which activated the miraculous recovery of the Japanese economy. About that time, the Housing Loan Corporation inaugurated the housing loan system to help finance the required funds for housing construction, thus paving the way for housing construction that covered most of the raid-devastated zones by around 1955. The population of the city area of Tokyo then exceeded the prewar high to reach 7 million (equivalent to the projected population of the city of Tokyo at the time of the postquake reconstruction).

The inflow of farm village population to major cities continued, and the average income level of urban worker households surpassed the farm household income level during the so-called Jinmu boom. (Jinmu was the alleged first Emperor of Japan, thus implying that the boom was the largest ever since the advent of the Japanese history.) Of course, the young laborers who came from rural farm villages to Tokyo lacked the financial resources to buy housing land for building their own houses; they needed rental places. To meet the requirements of these laborers wooden apartment houses were built along the Yamate Loop Line. They offered one-room apartments and common-use kitchens and washrooms, provided poor sunlight and ventilation, and were built side by side in limited land spaces, thus encouraging the spread of fire. Such wooden apartment houses mushroomed through the late 1950s and the early 1960s, and in 1970 nearly 40 percent of all households in the twenty-three-ward area in Tokyo were said to live in rental houses—mainly these wooden units. Large corporations built houses for their employees, and local governments also built rental houses for low-income households, with the former having a share of around 10 percent and the latter about 5 percent in Tokyo. However, the share of house-owning households in Tokyo was still around 45 percent, higher than the prewar figure. Because the house and land rents were frozen under the Land and House Rent Control Ordinance throughout the wartime and postwar years, and because postwar inflation was rampant, landowners stopped supplying rental houses and asked their tenants to purchase their plots and houses.

About that time, strong demands for better houses were made by the tenants of cheap wooden apartment buildings and corporate rental houses, which thus rapidly expanded demand for housing land in the suburbs of Tokyo. In the late 1940s large suburban farms of nonresident landowners were split through the Agrarian Land Reform into small plots under the individual ownership of tenant farmers, which thus scaled down the average farm size of individual farm households. Full-time farmers were troubled by the improper size of their farms in relation to their household labor force and farming machines and were eager to expand their operational size. They therefore had no reason to sell their land. Among the part-time farmers were those who may have thought about selling their farmland to earn money for building their own houses or starting new businesses but who hesitated to actually sell even fragmentary spaces—unless the prices were obviously lucrative—since such transactions made smaller their already small farm plots. The need for more farmland and the need for more housing land became thus incompatible with each other in the suburbs of major cities.

Land Use Planning on the Basis of the National Capital Sphere Redevelopment Act

In response to the rise of such rival demands, the National Capital Sphere Redevelopment Act was enacted in 1956 for the purpose of implementing a land use plan to cover not only the twenty-three-ward area of Tokyo but also the so-called National Capital Sphere as a whole; the First National Capital Sphere Redevelopment Plan was compiled in 1958. Classifying the National Capital Sphere into Town Areas, Suburban Areas, and Urbanization Areas, the plan initially aimed at containing the tendency of urbanization within the Town Areas (that is, the twenty-three-ward area of Tokyo plus Musashino City and its already urbanized adjacent areas in Yokohama, Kawasaki, Mitaka, and Kawaguchi cities). The Suburban Areas spread around the Town Areas, where the plan was designed to discourage housing land development to protect existing farmland. The Urbanization Areas stretched outside the Suburban Areas (within a range of 50 to 100 km from the city center), into which the plan was intended to lead urban population with a view to more or less slowing down the projected population growth in the Town Areas.

It was evident that this plan was modeled after the redevelopment plans of major cities in other advanced industrial countries, especially the Greater London Plan of 1944 by Sir Patrick Abercrombie. The Japanese plan copied the Greater London Plan in its approach of limiting the acreage of the Town Areas to around 90,000 hectares, surrounded with a total of about 600,000 hectares of Greenbelts, while absorbing the increasing population inflow in the National Capital Sphere into the so-called New Towns (the Urbanization Areas in the plan). With the population density assumed at around 130 persons per hectare in the Town Areas, this plan expected to accommodate approximately 12 million persons in 90,000 hectares within these areas while keeping the population density below 20 persons per hectare in the Suburban Areas so that about 13 million persons could be accommodated in a total of 600,000 hectares. (With an estimated future population of around 3 million in the Urbanization Areas added, the plan estimated the future population of the entire National Capital Sphere at around 28 million). The ideal at that time was to distinctly differentiate the Town Areas and the farm areas surrounding the towns.

Tokyo in the High Economic Growth Period

The entry of the Japanese economy into its high-growth stage in the early 1960s witnessed the transfer of the labor force from primary industry to secondary and tertiary industries. This interindustrial labor force transfer at the same time gave rise to an interregional population movement. Population influx into the National Capital Sphere continued intensively in the years surrounding the Tokyo Olympic games in 1964.

For instance, in the ten years following 1960 the share of labor force in the primary industry against the national total decreased from 33 to 19 percent, compared to share increases from 29 to 34 percent in the secondary industry and from 38 to 47 percent in the tertiary industry. In the same period, the share of population in the three major metropolitan spheres—Tokyo, Chubu (around Nagoya), and Kinki (including Kyoto, Osaka, and Kobe)—in comparison to the national total also rose from 45 to 51 percent.

One of the main causes for Japanese heavy and chemical industries reaching their current high levels of growth despite almost complete reliance on overseas resources for the supply of industrial raw materials is the fact that Japan could purchase resources from any supply sources in the world at low prices while decreasing freight costs by using larger freighters. The use of large-size freighters was made possible by the improvement of port and harbor facilities from public funds.

Back in the Tokugawa era, large cities in Japan were already located mostly close to the estuaries of large rivers, with agricultural production developing in their alluvial hinterlands and market access provided by means of navigation. After the Meiji revolution, the construction of modern port and harbor facilities was staged to replace the pre-Meiji facilities around these large cities, and the development of modern port and harbor facilities there helped to further expand such cities. Consequently, many large cities and adjacent ports and harbor facilities developed in close integration. It should also be noted that the development of coastal industrial zones in and around major metropolitan areas in postwar Japan was supported by large public fund appropriations.

Thus, Japanese major cities were attractive for the siting of industrial facilities in relation to access of raw materials. However, their attraction should also be noted in terms of market access. For instance, as of 1960, when the Japanese economy entered the initial orbit of high growth, the eight most urbanized prefectures—Tokyo, Kanagawa, Chiba, Saitama, Aichi, Osaka, Hyogo, and Fukuoka—shared 39 percent of the national population but 53 percent of national income and 61 percent of amount of investment in tangible fixed assets in manufacturing industry, thus evidencing a strong demand for goods in cities. Not only resources-reliant industries but also marketing-oriented factories sought siting locations close to major cities.

According to the regional industrial input/output analysis for 1960 (which was made by the Ministry of International Trade and Industry), the Kanto Region's manufacturing industry production heavily relied on demand from the same region; its exceedingly high reliance was almost equivalent to the National Capital Sphere's. In other words, the spin-off effect of manufacturing industry production in the Kanto Region in creating demand for other manufacture industry production in the region was superior to other regions. Since the share of the amount of industrial shipment in the Kanto Region compared to the national total was 32 percent—thus surpassing 25 percent for the Kinki Region, 16 percent for the Tokai Region, 3 percent for the Hokkaido Region, 3 percent for the Tohoku Region, 7 percent for the Chugoku Region, 2 percent for the Shikoku Region, and 7 percent for the Kyushu Region—it is conceivable that in the Kanto Region industrial production led to more industrial production and the siting of a plant led to more plant siting.

The concentration of capital in major cities gave rise to the concentration of population, since the concentration of capital there led to the expansion of production and the accompanying expansion of demand for labor, thus raising the wages in major cities over the wage level in farm villages.

With the outbreak of the Korean War as the turning point, the industrial level of war-devastated postwar Japan started upward; it recovered its prewar level as early as 1953 and continued to speed upward thereafter. Accordingly, the income level of urban worker households caught up with the income level of farm household and has since stayed that way. Since the family members per urban worker household was less than that of farm household, the per capita income ratio of the former was already 10 as against 6 for the latter around 1960, thus showing a notable income dislocation between urban workers and rural farmers.

This does not mean that Japanese agricultural technology was at a standstill. Owing to the farmers' ardent initiative for production following the Agrarian Land Reform and their accumulation of capital, they steadily increased productivity and raised the production level of 1960 about 30 percent higher than the prewar level. Still, the income gap between agriculture and nonagricultural industries expanded because the speed of the latter's annual growth was much faster. Agricultural income in 1960 was 11 percent of the total national income, though the agricultural labor force represented 30 percent of the whole labor force. Therefore, farmers sought more income from nonagricultural sources in order to catch up with the rising national income standard, while the nonagricultural sectors needed more labor transferred from agriculture to maintain growth.

Most of labor outflow from primary industry was absorbed into secondary industry (such as metals and machinery industries) and tertiary industry, both of which were mainstays of the economic growth of postwar Japan. Because these growing sectors were overwhelmingly in urban areas, interindustrial labor transfer also meant interregional labor transfer, thus increasing, for instance, the population of the National Capital Sphere from 18 million in 1960 to 24 million in 1970. Though the population of 24 million in the National Capital Sphere was as yet less than what the National Capital Sphere Redevelopment Plan had provided for, it should be noted that the intensive concentration of population in the suburban areas adjoining the already urbanized town areas had not been anticipated in the plan.

In fact, this plan was designed to minimize the development of suburban areas by limiting population influx therein. However, suburban farmers strongly opposed any such suburban land use control approach on the grounds that restraints on suburban land development would force suburban land prices downward; consequently, no land was designated as a Suburban Zone, though the zone had been expressly provided for in the National Capital Sphere Redevelopment Law.

The population inflow into the suburbs progressed without a break. The Japan Housing Corporation (which was inaugurated in 1955) started housing development and the construction of apartment house complexes for medium-income households in the suburban belts on a preferential basis, and private railways and many other private development corporations launched suburban housing land development. The mounting demand for suburban housing land finally led to the amendment of the Redevelopment Law in 1965, thus legally opening the door for developing suburban land in designated Suburban Development Zones. The focal point of urban problems at that time was the arrangement of commuters' traffic systems to accommodate train traffic congestion during rush hours. Both the Japan National Railways Corporation and private railway companies intensified their efforts to increase their train transportation capacity. These efforts, in turn, again facilitated the population flow out of the city areas into suburban belts.

Random housing development in the suburbs was accompanied by a multitude of deficiencies (to which I shall refer later in this book).

Constructing houses without making preliminary infrastructural arrangements for more public facilities such as city water and sewage services, roads, parks and schools increased pressure on local governmental finances. Critical voices against the suburbanization of the population rose, first of all, from among the local governments in the suburban belts. Since around 1965, they have opposed the siting of housing complexes by the Japan Housing Corporation and other public housing entities and thus have opposed the central government's housing supply policy.

Finally, with a view to working out a legal system to arrange a framework against random urbanization, the City Planning Law was substantially amended in 1968. The newly revised law classified the Town Planning Area into the Urbanization Promotion Area (UPA) (which is a target for positive urbanization) and the Urbanization Control Area (UCA) (where housing development is in principle barred from authorization). The zoning to designate the UPA and the UCA was implemented by the prefectural governments within the National Capital Sphere in 1970. As mentioned in Chapter 1, a total of about 320,000 hectares of UPA were designated in the Tokyo, Kanagawa, Chiba, and Saitama prefectures.

The total of 320,000 hectares designated is 3.6 times as large as the 90,000 hectares planned for the Town Areas under the prescribed National Capital Sphere Redevelopment Plan of 1955. It is also about 7 times the 47,000 hectares called for under the Tokyo city plan in the late 1920s following the Great Earthquake and 53 times as large as the 6,000 hectares that Akimasa Yoshikawa proposed for Tokyo in the early years of the Meiji era. The average population density in the UPA is 63 persons per hectare, thus falling well below the 100 to 150 persons per hectares that was projected in earlier Japanese city plans; indeed, there are criticisms to the effect that the current UPA is larger than needed. However, all the efforts to contain the tendency for urbanization within a limited area so far have ended in failure. Even at the time of the rezoning of 1970 and its review thereafter, landowners pushed to expand the UPA.

The most practical approach for an analysis of housing land supply and demand in the National Capital Sphere therefore is to study the situation within the UPA under the City Planning Law, which is discussed in Chapter 3.

Section 2. Development of the Real Estate Business[3]

Japanese real estate dealers are positioned between landowners and end users. Even when the housing land suppliers are the actual landowners—that is, farmer households, as described in the following chapters—the real estate dealers would also conceivably affect the volume of land supply and the shape of the cities in one way or another.

Whenever a city starts developing outward into suburbs, real estate dealers and developers intensify their activities. In Japan the first of such times occurred at the beginning of this century when the private railway companies stepped up their efforts to construct suburban lines in response to the suburbanization of urban population. Among these, the Minomo-Arima Electric Railway (later Hankyu Corporation) and the Mekaba Electric Railway (later Tokyu Corporation) were incorporated primarily for profit from housing development. When company stocks of the Minomo-Arima Electric Railway Company were initially issued in 1907, a large number of shares remained unpaid and turned into unclaimed stocks; the company's ability to pay as a railway firm had been uncertain because population along the planned line had not yet developed. Then Ichizo Kobayashi, the newly appointed president of the corporation, worked out a new management policy for advancing housing development in tandem with railway expansion so that expected profits could be integrated with railway operations. Based on this management policy, the Hankyu Corporation has since traditionally advanced housing developments (for instance, at Ikeda, Toyonaka, Takarazuka, and Ashiya) along its own railway lines in the outskirts of Osaka and Kobe cities. The Mekaba Electric Railway Company was initially inaugurated as the transportation branch of the Denen Toshi (Garden City) Company, which Eiichi Shibusawa had incorporated for suburban housing land development. It was later incorporated as an independent railway company. Actually, however, the housing developments at Senzoku, Denen-Chofu, and Ookayama and the Mekaba line operation were integrally advanced. The business strategy of planning new railway lines along with housing land development has been followed by the current Tokyu Corporation and is evident in the extension of the Oimachi line (current Denen-Toshi Line) after World War II.

The other private railway companies, including those that were established by electric power companies for the purpose of using surplus electricity, also developed housing land along their railways in the period of population suburbanization in the 1920s. Among these, Hanshin Electric Railway in the Osaka region and the Seibu Railway Company in the Tokyo region were especially notable in that they launched large housing development projects, respectively, in Nishinomiya and Sagisu in suburbs of Osaka and Mejiro and Oizumi in suburbs of Tokyo.

The initial operations of suburban railway companies inevitably experienced financial difficulties because limited rate revenues from relatively small numbers of passengers contrasted with enormous outlays for fixed capital. It is economically reasonable for such a company to purchase land along the planned railway line while land prices are still cheap prior to its opening to traffic and to sell developed land at higher prices so that the earned marginal profit can supplement the return from railway operations. As the suburban population in newly developed areas increases, the company can expect more passenger revenue. Private railway company operation is a kind of regional monopoly business, and it is not pressed by competition with other companies. Private businesses are, of course, not permitted to operate in the red and prefer as much profit as feasible to advance multilateral business operations, including department stores at major terminals. These are some of the reasons that many railway-based housing developers operate in the real estate business.

If a private railway company purchases untapped lands in an attempt to monopolize development profit out of expected land price increases following the opening of a new line, however, it would be sure to face hostile reactions from landowners along the planned new line. What is more, a private railway company often lacks sufficient funds to purchase land in large acreage after investing available funds in the railway construction. For this reason, the company may come to consider purchasing only a part of required land in order to launch a land readjustment project on the basis of joint venture with other neighboring landowners, thus sharing the housing land development costs as well as development profits with such landowners. This was the formula that Eiichi Shibusawa initially tried in the Denen Toshi Development Project and that the Tokyu Corporation has since traditionally followed.

A private railway company may be forced into housing development in order to support its railway operation, but it must initially find itself short of funds for full development. The private railway companies in the years during and immediately after World War II were unable to prevent other minor real estate developers from earning good profits out of small-size housing development works by taking advantage of land price rises along newly constructed lines.

However, with housing land demand steadily increasing in the suburban areas following the entry of the Japanese economy into its high-growth period after 1960, as did the number of motor vehicles, and the upturn of land prices continued even without the construction of new railways or land readjustment projects. This encouraged traditional real estate service companies that had been in the prewar zaibatsu groups (giant family trusts that characterized prewar Japan's economic structure—such as Mitsubishi Estate company and Mitsui Real Estate Development—to stage large-scale housing land development projects, though they had earlier limited operations to the management of rental office buildings and commercial land plots. Among the residential house building contractors who grew in response to massive demand for residential houses in the postwar years were those who opted for housing land development with ready-to-live houses provided in newly developed land plots. They were called private developers, and they started large-scale housing development projects in newly acquired woodlands on diluvial uplands, avoiding farmlands that farmers were reluctant to sell for fear of reducing their efficient sizes of operation.

Real Estate Business in the High Economic Growth Period

In the early 1960s land prices swung upward, and the annual rate of land price rises exceeded 20 percent on average in the National Capital Sphere. Since an annual price rise at 20 percent or more was much higher than the average commercial bank rate, real estate was generally accepted as the most profitable investment whenever surplus funds were available. Therefore, trust banks and other financial institutions that had long-term funds competed to offer loans to real estate business promoters. Even companies in the other businesses organized real estate departments within their organizations or inaugurated real estate companies separately in an attempt to gain windfall profits by holding newly purchased land for some time before its sale at a higher price (this type of tactics was called *land rolling*), without actually entering the area of housing land development. At this time the myth about profit-bearing land became deeply rooted among the Japanese people, and fetishism about land dominated the Japanese mentality. These companies hunted for land more out of this fetishism than out of actual need. The number of curtilage-and-structure trade licensed firms increased to around 36,000 in 1973 from only 9,000 throughout Japan in 1966. The joke at the time was that "All the population of Japan is real estate dealers." The goal of real estate dealers to earn good profits at that time was based on buying up as much acreage as possible. Since the annual percentage rise of land prices was higher than the bank rate, dealers borrowed as much as permissible from banks to buy land and expected large profits in proportion to the period of holding. They therefore sold acreage only to earn cash for annual interest and tax payments. It seemed as though the highest future profits could be guaranteed if the acreage of land in one's possession was largest. At the same time, because any company registered land assets at cost in its balance sheet, it could have the value of these assets increasing along with the rise of market price, thus pressing the per share price of its capital stock upward in cases where it was a company listed on the securities exchange market and providing it with the means of easier funds procurement from the capital market.

For these reasons, private companies spared no efforts to expand the acreage of land in their possession. Consequently, speculation-based demand invited more speculative demand, definitely surpassing the limited supply of untapped land and thus skyrocketing the land prices. On the other hand, as was referred to earlier, farmers as the original owners of untapped land did not always want to sell their land. In addition, farmers in need of cash income could raise what they needed by selling lesser acreage because of the rise in land prices. Therefore, despite their strong desire for increasing the land in their possession, companies could not acquire land as easily as they hoped for, which led them to buy untapped land even where no actual demand for housing seemed likely.

From 1972 to 1973 a huge amount of foreign currencies suddenly flowed into Japan from speculative foreign exchange transactions conducted during the transition from the fixed exchange rate system to the floating system, thus causing so-called excessive liquidity in the Japanese money market. Against this sort of background, *Building a New Japan* incited private businesses to hunt for and buy land far from urban areas. Private businesses at that time were said to have bought hundreds of thousands of hectares across the country.

Section 3. Land Use Control

Distinction between UPA and UCA

As was explained earlier, there still is much land available for conversion into housing lands in the UPA in the National Capital Sphere. The actual situation is determined, in part, by how the UPA and the UCA are classified under the City Planning Law, which classifies the city planning area into two major categories—the Urbanization Promotion Area (UPA) and the Urbanization Control Area (UCA). UPA is defined as "the zone where towns have already been formed and the zone where urbanization will be sought on the preferential and planned basis within around 10 years." As the law operates, the zone where towns have already been formed is deemed to consist of the following areas:

1. Areas with a population of 5,000 persons or more, with population density—calculated on the basis of the population census target areas or of every 20 to 30 hectares sites within the area—not less than 40 persons per hectare.

2. Areas adjoining areas described in (1) above that contain land units, each not exceeding 50 hectares and each having a total of infrastructure built plots and similar plots not less than one-third of the land units.

3. Areas adjoining areas described in either (1) or (2) above, where housing construction or housing land development is actually ongoing and that are expected to fall into the category of (1) or (2) within about ten years.

The zone "where urbanization will be sought on the preferential and planned basis within around 10 years" means

4. Areas not exceeding 100 hectares surrounded by areas where formation of towns is nearly completed.

The law also provides that any farmland group not less than 20 hectares and woodland group not less than 100 hectares must become part of the UCA, thus barring the presence of any such farmland or woodland group in the UPA. In other words, any potential land convertible into housing land within a UPA is either sprawling farmland (at maximum 20 hectares) or woodland (at maximum not exceeding 100 hectares). These small individual land units, however, add up to the large acreages when combined for the National Capital Sphere.

As is obvious from Figure 2.1., which shows the distribution of farmland in Nerima Ward, Tokyo, farmlands have been extremely fragmented except for the somewhat integrated cluster in the northwestern corner. These farmland clusters, each not exceeding 1 hectare, contain 60 percent of the total number of farms but hold only 19 percent of the acreage. On the other hand, farmland clusters larger than 10 hectares equal only 3 percent of the total but hold 25 percent of acreage. There is no farmland group exceeding 20 hectares.

Such fragmented land units are even further subdivided for conversion into housing land plots, thus causing the so-called sprawling, which creates one of the most complicated problems for city planning. The term *sprawl* has been used extensively since World War II to describe the random expansion of an urban city into suburban farm areas; the term *diffusion* was common before that. As the original meaning of the word suggests, the postwar expansion of cities in other advanced industrial countries occurred as residential houses, stores, and even factories

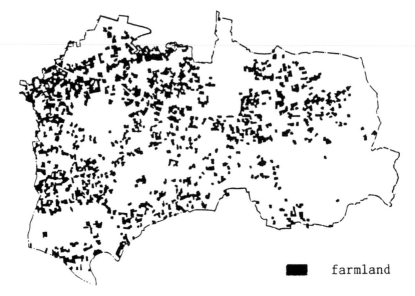

farmland

Figure 2.1. *Distribution of farmland in Nerima Ward.* (Source: *Urban Environment Research Insitute, Land Bureau, National Land Agency, "Survey of Available Farmland for Utilization in the Urbanization Promotion Areas"* (1977).

spread along highways from midtown into suburban farming areas. This phenomenon is normally called *ribbon-urbanization.*

In Japan, however, the urbanization of suburban farm areas usually does not progress in the shape of ribbons. Unlike in Europe and the United States, farmland in Japan is small, and individual farmers hold arable plots scattered over a fairly wide area, which facilitates land sales one by one. Under these circumstances, urbanization cannot proceed consistently within integrated city planning. What has occurred in Japan may better be represented by the word *diffusion* or *encroachment* rather than *sprawl.*

National Land Use Planning Act

Institutional arrangements for the control of land use in Japan have made remarkable progress. The City Planning Law was substantially revised in 1968, the Agriculture Promotion Area Arrangement Law was enacted in 1969 with a view to facilitating planned land use in farm areas, and the National Land Use Planning Act was enacted in 1974 for the purpose of advancing planned land use throughout the country. The National Land Use Planning Act also provides for state legislation for comprehensive planning, and oversees the Forest Act. the Natural

Park Law, and the Natural Environment Preservation Law in addition to the City Planning Law and the Agriculture Promotion Area Arrangement Law. This law authorizes the government to develop a comprehensive countrywide plan for land use. Until its enactment, there had been no comprehensive land use plan in Japan that applied to both urban areas and farm villages, though land use had been controlled locally by separate plans for the City Plan Areas in urban regions and by the Land Improvement Plan Areas in agricultural regions.

Compared with the failed efforts to manage random land development under the Capital Sphere Redevelopment Act (see Section 1 of this chapter), the enactment of the National Land Use Planning Act marked a leap forward in the progress of the land planning system. This act was developed to integrally plan land use in association with the revised City Planning Law, which provided for the zoning of the UCA, and the Agriculture Promotion Arrangement Law, which limited the conversion of farmland into housing land.

A reasonable land use plan is the indispensable prerequisite to land policy, and Japan now has a well-arranged system of land use planning. However, its mechanism for planning land use is the control of land use: That is, Japan prohibits specified forms of land use within designated areas, and administrative penalties—such as destruction, penal servitude, and fines—are prescribed against those who violate the prohibition. In this way, land use can be limited to a certain extent. On the other hand, neither the National Land Use Planning Act nor the City Planning Law has the power to positively encourage specific forms of land use. For instance, most of the farmland and woodland within UPAs have been designated for the exclusive residence zones where the building code regulates. The law cannot force landowners to desist from leaving land vacant or from using it for agriculture. Because the control system of land use cannot advance the conversion of farmland and woodland into housing land, it can never effectively control land prices, no matter how many regulatory arrangements are provided, how reasonable the land use plan is, or how carefully the control system of land use is integrated with the plan.

Section 4. Land Expropriation

Eminent Domain

While control over land use may act against undesirable use of land, land expropriation achieves desirable use. The history of the eminent domain system is much longer than the system of control over land use. Though Article 27 of the Imperial Constitution (1889) of prewar Japan provided that "the proprietary rights of the Japanese subjects to land shall never be infringed," the first Eminent Domain Law of Imperial Japan was also enacted in the same year, and it was replaced by more systematic legislation in 1900.

The main features of the Eminent Domain Law of 1900 can be analyzed by examining its criteria for determining whether or not to support a public project for which the law applied and its method for calculating compensations payable to landowners who were affected by its application.

This law brought under its control virtually any public project by categorically prescribing such projects as "any project which concerns national defense and/or other military matters" and even as "any project which shall be implemented by the State, Prefecture, City, Township, Village or other Public Entity for the purpose of public use." The public nature of such projects, the law declared were to be certified as follows: "the competent Minister shall certify any project for authorizing to take or use of land therewith"; "however, any project that concerns military secrets shall be not bound to the foregoing." It also provided no criteria for certifying the minister's competency. Under this law, the power to expropriate land dominated private ownership of land and was virtually free from legal restriction.

The Expropriation Examination Committee, which was authorized to decide on compensation, consisted of the prefectural governor as chairman and six members—three members appointed by the minister from among officers in senior-level civil service and the remaining three members elected from among honorary counsellors to the prefectural government. The committee was thus free from legislative check and control. This may explain why the amount of compensation was surprisingly low in the well-known case of the land expropriation in Yanaka Village (the most serious application of the law in the history of the country) compared with those in other neighboring areas (where the law had been enforced for the construction of flood control cisterns along the Watarase River). The court later ordered the prefectural government to make additional compensations.

Article 13 of the New Constitution of postwar Japan (promulgated in 1946) reads: "All of the people shall be respected as individuals. Their right to life, liberty, and the pursuit of happiness shall, to the extent that it does not interfere with the public welfare, be the supreme consideration in legislation and in other governmental affairs." The right to the pursuit of happiness was emphasized instead of the right to property because in both the United States of America and Japan the right to property was accepted, at least for some time, as subordinate to or a part of the right to the pursuit of happiness.

The right to property is also recognized under the Japanese constitution, Article 29 of which reads: "The right to own or to hold property is inviolable." This clause, however, is immediately followed by "Property rights shall be defined by law, in conformity with the public welfare." In other words, if the right to own or hold land is incompatible with the public welfare, it must submit to the public welfare and not vice versa. Article 29 further states: "Private property can be taken for public use upon just compensation therefor."

The public welfare and the amount of just compensation are determined by procedures stipulated by the Eminent Domain Law. Based on the philosophy of the new constitution, the Eminent Domain Law of 1951 was compiled as the revised version of the Law of 1900. Under the 1951 law (1) the range of qualified agencies was explicitly defined; (2) the descriptions of procedures for the certification of specific projects were accurately worded; (3) the name of the Expropriation Examination Committee changed to the Expropriation Committee, and the appointment of its members was bound to the prefectural assembly's approval; (4) rights coming under expropriation were more clearly defined, and provisions governing compensation for losses were more accurately worded.

Article 3 of the Eminent Domain Law lists over forty classified types of agencies that are governed by this law because of their public nature. Among these are the "management by the state, local autonomy, Japan Housing Corporation or a local housing corporation of a housing complex with more than 50 housing units affiliated for the purpose of renting or transferring such units to the housing needy persons in the Exclusive Residential Area, as provided for in Chapter Two of the City Planning Law." Since this law recognizes the public nature of housing land supply, it is feasible that the law may be employed for the purpose of converting farmland or woodland into housing land. The law is insufficient to control the housing land prices in major urban regions because of the problem of just compensation.

With respect to just compensation, academic polemics in Japan centered on the constitutionality of the postwar Agrarian Land Reform. Under Agrarian Land Reform, the government purchased on a compulsory basis all the tenanted farm plots of nonresident landowners and the tenanted farm plots of resident landowners exceeding 1 chobu (4 chobu in Hokkaido) per owner (1 chobu equals approximately 1 hectare or 2.5 acres) and sold these to nonlanded tenant farmers. In this way, 2 million hectares of farmland, one-third of Japan's total, was transferred from former landowners from the first purchase in March 1947 to the sixth in July 1950. Moreover, 450,000 hectares of grassland and

1.32 million hectares of wild land had also been transferred.

The government's purchase price was calculated on the basis of the amount of presumed earnings as of November 1945, which was derivable from the difference between the officially controlled rice price and the rice production cost at that time—with the then prevailing rate of interest on the government bonds used as a scale to estimate the net worth of land as a capital asset. This calculation formula was reasonably justifiable at that time, but the calculated purchase price itself was substantially depreciated in the course of later hyperinflation. Therefore, the former landowners sued on the complaint that the Law on Extraordinary Measures for Creating Landed Farmers, which led to determining the unreasonably low purchase prices, violated Article 29, Paragraph 3, of the constitution providing for just compensation. The National Supreme Court ruled in December 1953 that the purchase price at the time of the Agrarian Land Reform was incompatible with "just compensation" as provided for in the constitution.

In connection with this case, academic debate over the interpretation of "just compensation" focused on a perfect compensation theory and an appropriate compensation theory. The former called for perfect compensation for losses arising from restriction on titles to property for the sake of public purpose. The latter was not clear about the definition of "appropriate," though many of the supporters of this theory claimed that "appropriate" does not always need to be "perfect." The perfect compensation theory involved a decisive error in terms of practicality, however, because it is not feasible to compensate all the losses that a claimant claims on the basis of subjective allegations. The view that any loss can be compensated in one way or another is based on an approach that diverges from the subjective position of the claimant. A standard other than the subjective allegation of the claimant to determine the amount of compensation would lead to compensation that does not deserve the name of perfect compensation. The compensation in this case should be called appropriate compensation because the standard itself determines a priori the losses disqualified for compensation from those eligible.

The arguments over the advantages of perfect compensation and appropriate compensation were futile. It was more important to specify the losses that are qualified for compensation and those that are not. The details of just compensation are neither forever invariable nor derivable from a deductive logic because the concept itself is positioned at the point of balance between individual right and public welfare.

The current Eminent Domain Law stipulates that "with the market prices of similar land plots in its neighborhood taken into account, an appropriate price should be compensated for the land under expropriation." This stipulation stands for the so-called principle of market price and is designed to avoid possible inequity between the landowners who are expropriated of land and those who remain unaffected. However, as long as the public authorities exercise land expropriation by paying market prices for untapped land, they cannot use this power as an instrument to lower the market price level because the determining factor is market, not government.

It may be feasible to invalidate the principle of market price in the Eminent Domain Law, but such an action would give renewed dominance to the bureaucracy. With administrative discretion permitted in quantifying just compensation, bureaucrats might revive a situation where they can act as arbitrarily as their predecessors in the prewar Ministry of Home Affairs had done in the case of cisterns along the Watarase River.

In this respect, it is also feasible under the Eminent Domain Law to legally control land prices, including general transaction prices. For instance, the National Land Use Planning Act provides for a system of designated Price Controlled Areas for the purpose of freezing land prices. It authorizes the prefectural governor to designate the price controlled area and to freeze all the land prices therein at the level of publicly announced land prices at the time of the designation and to permit the price increases thereafter only in correspondence to the range of increases in the consumer price index. This system can be most effective when it is implemented in a limited area—for instance, around a newly opened railway station or an interchange of a newly built speedway. However, it is not realistic to designate as the control area all of the suburban zones adjoining a major urban area where demand for land is strong. Even if such an area is designated, the result could be widespread black marketeering.

Public institutions are not authorized to pay higher unit prices than the publicly announced land prices for the acquisition of public-use land, but they often add extras to the cost for moving structures and to the estimated prices of planted trees. Where private housing companies sell ready-to-live-in houses, they normally notify the local authorities that prices for the plots are close to the publicly announced land prices, but they actually ask users to pay higher prices for the houses in package with the plots.

Eminent domain is an instrument that can best serve its purpose of achieving desired use of land when it is applied to cases with a minority of opponents, an extensive majority of people who support the objective of the planned project, and a majority of affected landowners who accept the formula for compensation. It is not suitable to a large area that, for instance, might reach nearly one-quarter of the total UPAs.

There is sometimes heard what can be called demand for a second agrarian land reform in order to settle the problems of housing land price; however, it is impossible to apply land appropriation selectively to farmland in the UPA without violating the principle of equality under law.

Land Replotting ("Readjustment")

The original purpose of land expropriation is not to repress land prices but to realize the desired use of land, including public-use spaces, with a view to building a better housing environment. Land replotting within the framework of land readjustment can also be considered a variety of expropriation. Under eminent domain, private land ownership is to be terminated with compensation paid in exchange, while in land replotting, substitute land is to be offered in exchange for the termination of private land ownership. In both cases, the private land ownership is to be terminated for the sake of public purposes.

The first law in Japan concerning land replotting was the Arable Land Readjustment Law (enacted in 1899). Initially, the law aimed at replotting paddyfields units of a single landowner or at most several landowners jointly and to arrange irrigation and drainage, thus meeting the landed class's requirement for more farm rent. However, the 1909 revision of this law authorized the Arable Land Readjustment Associations, as main promoters of land readjustment projects, to enforce the planned replotting on the basis of the association's resolution, even when half of the landowners opposed the project within the plan area, thus creating forced cooperation.

The Arable Land Readjustment Law obligated the landowners in the target area to contribute required public land units without compensation to the state in exchange for free transfer of such pre-replotting public units as common-use lanes and waterways. Though this law provided no specific stipulation about the contribution rate due to the replotting, it provided for a rule that the total amount of land tax on the target area would be maintained at the same level as before the replotting, even in cases where the post-replotting acreage therein exceeded the pre-replotting acreage. (Usually, the post-replotting acreage exceeded the pre-replotting acreage in the target area due to the relocation of boundaries and the discovery of extra space over the registered acreage through the certifying land survey.) This facilitated land readjustment by prearranging many favorable conditions for landowners.

The Arable Land Readjustment Law was enacted, of course, with farm areas as its main target, but as mentioned earlier, replotting had been advanced in the suburban areas under this law in the beginning of this century. At that time, the average contribution rate through replotting was around 20 percent.

However, the Arable Land Readjustment Law was made applicable mutatis mutandis to the public projects for town area readjustments in virtually all the quake-damaged areas in Tokyo following the enactment of the Special City Planning law in the wake of the 1923 earthquake. More compulsory features were incorporated into such readjustment projects, and local administrative offices acted as the main promoters. These projects thus differed from the arable land readjustment projects that had been initiated by landowners.

Following the enactment of the Land Readjustment Law in 1954, land readjustment projects have been given an important place in city planning schemes. The opponents of land readjustment often regard the law as a policy instrument for expropriating land without compensation, which the Japanese constitution prohibits. Private land space reduction is certainly inevitable in the land readjustment formula, since such space reduction under the name of communal contribution is compulsory and is a measure for creating public land such as roads and parks. However, such contribution is, in the opinion of proponents of this formula, not at all land seizure without compensation or in violation of the constitution because it will be fully recovered with the rise of land values caused by land readjustment. Beyond that, land readjustment is the best method for arranging roads and parks for all citizens in a housing area.

These two contradictory approaches seem unlikely to find a point of mutual compromise, because of the following facts: (1) In the ordinary case of land expropriation, landowners who offer their property for the construction of a highway can duly expect their counterpart gains from the future price rises of their land spaces along the highway; and (2) the inhabitants of houses with small plots in the target area of land readjustment, however, cannot expect such gains from the land price rises unless they sell their own houses together with the plots.

Even if the public sector acquires public spaces by expropriation instead of replotting based on private land reduction, the cost of purchasing the required spaces would eventually be borne by many unspecified taxpayers. In cases where the expected users of public units are limited to the inhabitants in the neighborhood and where such users bear the cost individually prorated to the benefits they should receive, the total amount of their payments would still be close to the cost for the replotting. In view of the benefits to be derived from replotting as compared with the land expropriation, the claim that the land readjustment violates the constitution cannot be supported.

Section 5. Land Tax

Real Property Tax

Taxation on land has a long history. The land tax revision in the initial years of the Meiji era provided the imperial government with a solid financial foundation after the Meiji restoration. However, in 1949 the Shoup mission's recommendation (on the invitation of General MacArthur, supreme commander of the occupation forces) proposed a drastic change in the public finance system of postwar Japan, and there followed the establishment of the local tax system.

The primary purpose of the Shoup recommendation was to rehabilitate Japanese finances after the confusion that followed World War II. However, its important objective was to establish a system of local public financial autonomy, something that had been virtually nonexistent in prewar Japan. In Shoup's philosophy, local autonomy—especially at the municipal level—is the foundation of democracy: It is an indispensable condition for democracy that independent revenue sources be established free of the central government's intervention. Based on this philosophy, Shoup proposed the inhabitant tax and the property tax. This book is concerned only with the property tax.

Before the Shoup recommendation, there had been a land tax and a house tax, with most of the revenues therefrom attributed to the municipalities. However, Shoup combined the land and house taxes with the depreciable assets tax and named them the property tax. The rate was 1.75 percent of the value at market price and was the mainstay of the municipal revenues. It now is called real property tax, and its rate has decreased to 1.4 percent with 0.7 percent upward allowance at the discretion of every municipality. To justify the real property tax as the center of the municipal revenue sources, Shoup made the following points:

1. Because this tax is easier to operate and involves fewer loopholes that allow tax evasion, it is well suited to small units of government, as is evident from the cases in Europe and North America where it has been the traditional revenue source.

2. The value of real property and the tax-bearing capacity of people who live there are nearly balanced under this tax. In addition, businesses in commercial quarters at the center of cities also bear the tax in exchange for the benefits they enjoy from local public services such as police protection, fire-brigade activities, roads, and parks.

3. The revenue from this tax increases in correspondence to inflation and thus is inflation-hedged.

Also included in the Shoup recommendations was a net worth tax to impose a progressive tax with rates from 0.5 percent to 2.5 percent on the personal property of an individual, including securities, paintings, and jewelery. To justify this tax, Shoup made the following two points:

1. Though the national tax system should be based on the progressive income tax, a high-rate tax on large income earners inevitably causes tax evasion. In order to prevent tax evasion, there should be a ceiling to limit the progressive rate. Taxation on personal property can decrease tax evasion while supplementing income tax in the area beyond the ceiling of its progressive rate.

2. Such taxation can also contribute to the better utilization of resources, since the wealthy class must pay for hoarding personal property.

Though the net worth tax was enforced as Shoup recommended, it was abolished several years after its implementation because personally owned property was difficult to determine. Generally speaking, land and housing were the largest sources of personal property in Japan. Thus the real property tax functions in place of the net worth tax to some extent.

With the enactment of the Local Taxes Law in 1949 following the enactment of the Local Finance Law in 1948, the financial foundation of local autonomy was firmly established. The assessed values of real property for taxation were appraised by specialist assessors in the municipalities, as had been proposed in the Shoup recommendation. Real property was assessed on the principle of ad valorem or appraisal by the market value, though depreciable assets were not reappraised by the market value after depreciation deduction. The only exception was farmland, which was subject to taxation on the basis of the legally fictitious prices, reflecting the fact that at that time farm products were subject to compulsory sale to the government at low prices and that farmland prices were legally determined in association with the Agrarian Land Reform.

By the middle of the 1960s the need for special rules for farmland had gradually decreased, which led to the revision of the Local Taxes Law in 1964. This revision applied the rule of ad valorem or appraisal by the market value to farmland and standardized the diverse criteria among municipalities for the assessment of land. As compared with actual transaction prices, the assessed land values at that time were said to be around one-quarter for farmland and woodland and around one-sixth for housing land. According to a trial calculation of the land tax under the revised law, the tax amounts on land were estimated to increase by 6.3 times for housing land, by 3 times for woodland, and 4.3 times for farmland as compared with before the revision.

With this in mind, the farmers' organizations and the opposition parties launched a resolute campaign against such radical tax increases, which led to a partial revision of the Local Taxes Law by the National Diet in March 1964. This revision provided for determining the 1964 land assessment as of the date of 1 January 1964 but adopting the FY 1963 rate for the tax on farmland. Furthermore, based on a recommendation by the Tax Council, an interim revision was made to the Local Taxes Law in 1966 to raise the amount of tax on housing land by 10 percent each year in cases where the newly assessed values of land were less than three times of the previous assessment, by 20 percent each year in cases where the newly assessed values were three times or more of the previous assessment and less than eight times thereof, and by 30 percent in cases where the newly assessed values were eight times or more of the previous assessment. In this revision, farmland was again excepted from the FY 1967 reassessment, with the amount of tax pegged to the 1963 level. These provisional measures continued until the end of 1972. Then, on the occasion of the 1973 reassessment, the tax system was revised to set the assessment standard of the taxable amount of private housing land plot at one-half of the appraised value, and the provisional measures were discontinued. In other words, the tax rates on such housing plots were legally halved.

With respect to farmland, the Supplementary Provisions of the Local Taxes Law were partially revised in March 1971. With this revision, farmlands in UPAs were classified into three classes: (1) Class A farmland's appraised unit value equaled or exceeded the average price of housing land plots in the same municipality or was not less than Yen 50,000; (2) Class B farmland's appraised unit value was below Yen 50,000 and not less than Yen 10,000 and, besides, below the average price of housing land in the same municipality and not less than one-half thereof; and (3) Class C farmland's appraised unit value was less than Class B farmland. Then, the Supplementary Provisions also provided for bringing the assessment of taxable value of farmland closer to the level of adjacent housing plots in a period of three years beginning with FY 1972 for Class A farmland, a period of four years beginning with FY 1973 for Class B farmland, and a period of five years beginning with FY 1976 for Class C farmland.

It was surprising that the above revision was approved in the National Diet session without sizable resistance. However, prior to its implementation in FY 1972, radical opposition surged up from among the farmers' organizations, despite the fact that only 2.5 percent of farmlands in UPAs were identified as Class A.

The development of this campaign demonstrates how the political parties in Japan are typically submissive to the pressure of farmers' votes and timid in advancing urban policy. Around mid-February, the Central Council of Agricultural Co-operative Associations and the National Chamber of Agriculture jointly held in Tokyo the National Conference of the Representatives of Agricultural Committees of Agricultural Co-op Associations to "oppose the market value taxation on farmland in UPAs," with a large number of invited Diet members from all political parties participating, and these Diet members were asked to individually pledge their support for the policy of the conference. This immediately led to the organization of the Diet Members' League for Farmland in UPAs (150 members) within the Liberal-Democratic Party, where farming-related members acted as its core. This pressure group ultimately succeeded in influencing the LDPs Policy Affairs Research Council to work out a policy that required the advisory councils to the municipal governments to exclude all of "farmlands which can be recognized as plots used for farming" from market value taxation.

In this process, all the opposition parties, the Japan Socialist Party, the Komei Party, the Japan Communist Party, and the Democratic-Socialist Party aligned their positions with the LDP, and the four opposition parties jointly submitted a proposal to the National Diet for postponing the newly enacted Supplementary Provisions of the Local Taxes Law—which provided for the implementation of the market value taxation on farmland in UPAs. The proposal was approved on 30 March 1973. Thus, the real property tax has been virtually invalid insofar as farmland is concerned.

Tax on Capital Gains

The Shoup recommendation proposed that the total amount of the capital gains from land be deemed as a taxable amount and that a tax be imposed by installments on the full amount over an appropriate length of years on the assumption that each installment is the capital gains accruing in every single year within the period. In spite of this proposal, the Japanese government continued the conventional one-half tax on capital gains—taxing only one-half of the total capital gains in the year when the gains accrued—which Shoup had earlier criticized as an absurd system encouraging speculation.

However, in response to the radical land price rises and accompanying speculative land purchases in the late 1960s, a review of the tax system on capital gains was made, which led to the implementation of the proportional tax on capital gains apart from the other income beginning with FY 1969. The tax rate was 10 percent (with 4 percent of inhabitant tax added) each in FY 1969, FY 1970, and FY 1971, with 5 percent (with 1 percent of inhabitant tax added) each added every other year thereafter.

The reasons for this decision to alleviate the tax burden were (1) that a too heavy tax on capital gains from land sales discourages landowners, especially landed farmers, from selling their plots and turns the land market more into a seller's market and (2) that under a progressive tax system, landowners would not sell land in large acreage but do so only in fragments.

This tax reduction on capital gains from land sales certainly increased not only land supply but also the number of high-income earners from land sale, according to the annually published list of high-income earners. Perhaps growing apprehensions over the mushrooming "land-based nouveaux riches" led the government in 1976 to discontinue the proportional tax on capital gains from land apart from the other incomes and to adopt a tax rate of 20 percent on the taxable amount of capital gains at Yen 20 million or less, while applying the ordinary progressive tax rates (in case the taxable amount exceeds Yen 20 million) on the excess together with other incomes on the grounds that three-quarters of that excess amount is inclusive in the ordinary income at the highest-income bracket. However, the government again changed this system, beginning in 1979, to apply the ordinary progressive tax rates on one-half, instead of three-quarters, of that excess. In addition, together with this change, a new system was introduced to apply the segregated proportional tax rates on capital gains, in case these accrued from the sales of farmland in UPAs in the major urban regions for housing land development, at 15 percent on the taxable amount not more than Yen 40 million and 20 percent on the taxable amount exceeding Yen 40 million. The land tax system has thereafter been revised virtually from year to year, thus building a reputation of being as fickle as a cat's eye. Such frequent changes of the land tax system are evidence that the government has had no firmly established logical response to the effects of the income tax on capital gains.

Real Estate Acquisition Tax

The Real Estate Acquisition Tax is a tax on the transfer of land and was one of the important revenue sources of prefectures before the end of World War II. However, its alleged importance notably declined after the Shoup recommendation criticized it as disruptive of the smooth distribution of real estate.

This tax is currently prefectural and taxable on the same assessment standard as the real property tax with the tax rate at 5 percent. Though the tax has nothing to do with the promotion of untapped land supply, it may depress land prices if it is substantially raised, since payment offsets the ability to pay of the buyers of such land. However, since the purpose of curbing land price rises is to secure better housing conditions for a given income level, a higher rate of this tax would act to push down not only land prices but also the ability to pay of its users. A heavy tax on land transactions is therefore undesirable land policy, as the Shoup recommendation earlier claimed.

Inheritance Tax

In compliance with the new Constitution and the Civil Code (revised in 1947), the inheritance tax system was radically changed. Before the revision of the Inheritance Tax Act in 1947 the tax was levied on the legal heir (usually the eldest son), and calculations were based on the total estimated value of the inherited property. Under the revision, the tax is to be levied on each heir based on the respectively estimated value of the inherited property. Here also Shoup's recommendation helped introduce a progressive scheme in order to prevent accumulation of wealth in a few people.

The rate of inheritance tax varies from 10 percent to 70 percent in accordance with the amount of taxable property after basic deductions for each heir and special deductions for the spouses of the deceased, which change with the length of period of the marriage status.

It should be noted that as the assessment standard for land property rises closer to the market value of land, the inheritance tax on land reaches a huge sum in the case of large landowners. The heir often must sell a part of the land in order to pay the tax. Therefore, it can be said that by upgrading the assessment standard closer to the market value of land, the inheritance tax is a progressive tax that reliably functions to increase the supply of untapped land.

However, this raises a question of equalizing the tax burden among taxpayers, if its application should be limited to the UPAs. If, on the other hand, the ad valorem assessment is applied even to farm areas, the aggregate of inheritance tax payments by full-time farmers would rise to a very high level, which might ruin full-time farmers in Japan because farmland prices have also substantially increased along with general land price rises throughout the country.

The principle of equal tax burden should be observed. Therefore, if reduction of the inheritance tax on farmland is justifiable only for full-time farmers for agricultural policy, a lesser rate of such tax should be considered for them in exchange for strict control against the conversion of their farmland into other uses, just as it is controlled in the areas currently under the Law for Arrangement of the Agriculture Promotion Area. Such control by itself can help protect existing farmland. In addition, stricter control of the conversions may help repress the price of farmland, thus conceivably preventing the inheritance tax on farmland from rising to a high level. However, such policy has not yet been applied.

A major criticism to the present land policy of Japan is that it lacks coordination between land use controls and land taxation. The confusion in property tax and inheritance tax of farmland in the UPAs is typical of this deficiency.

Notes

1. K. Horiuchi, *Toshi Keikaku to Yoto-Chiiki-Sei (City Planning and Segregated Zoning)* (Nishida Shoten, 1978). Shibata Tokue, *Nihon No Toshi Seisaku (Urban Policy in Japan)* (Yuhikaku, 1978), was also used as a reference book on city planning for Tokyo in the Meiji era.
2. Tokyo Municipal Government, *Teito Fukko Kukaku Seiri-Shi (Records of Land Readjustment for the Reconstruction of the Imperial Capital City)* (Tokyo Municipal Government, 1932).
3. Norio Gamachi, *Fudosan Gyokai (Real Estate Businesses)* (Tokyo: Kyoiku-sha, 1979).

3

Structure of the
Housing Land Market

Many people are unsatisfied with the explanation for increased land prices given by orthodox economists using supply and demand curves. In many cases, a shift of the demand or supply curve is given as the reason for a change in price, but this type of explanation is a tautology. The real questions to be answered are why and how the curves shifted. It is well known that demand for land was particularly strong during the period of rapid economic growth in the 1960s and the early years of the 1970s before the oil crisis. Without analyzing the supply side as well as the demand side, however, one cannot understand the actual cause of land price rises. This chapter analyzes the structure of the housing land market in the Tokyo area in the 1960s and the 1970s.

Section 1. Quantitative Analysis of Land Supply

The Concept of Housing Land Supply

If land was not short in absolute terms, as was shown in Chapter 1, then why did land prices continue rising year after year? In answering this question, I should point out that housing land supply could not catch up with rising demand in the 1960s and 1970s. Though the stock of land with a potential for conversion into housing land was large, actual conversion was limited. Figure 3.1. shows a flow chart of the main distribution routes of marketable land to the housing end users.

A typical case of the shortest distribution route is the purchase by either a public land developer such as the Japan Housing Corporation or a private real estate dealer of untapped land (farm and woodland) from a landowner or landowners (mainly farmers) for development

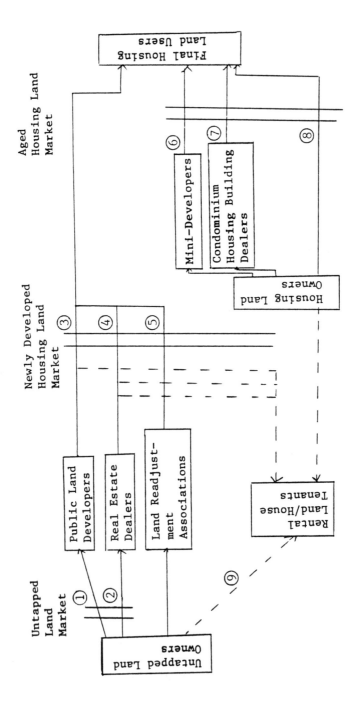

Figure 3.1. *Flow chart of commodity of land.*

into housing land and sale to end users. There also are cases where a land readjustment association is an organization of untapped landowners who develop their own land into housing land for sale to end users. These routes together form a housing land market. If sales in this market are traceable, it should be easy to determine the quantitative supply of housing land. However, there are other causes that contribute to the increase of the stock of housing land: An owner of untapped land may develop it into housing land by himself for rental as land or by building semidetached houses or apartment houses for rent. In addition, a public agency may develop its land and build housing. In the latter cases, the newly developed housing land is not subject to transactions and, therefore, it is difficult to calculate its share of the housing land market.

Moreover, among the housing plots already in stock, are those, especially among large plots, that are sold to minidevelopers and condominium housing building dealers who subdivide or redevelop such plots into smaller plots for sale to end users. Large plots also are sold without undergoing subdivision or redevelopment. The transactable plots in these three cases form what can be called a "pre-existing" housing land market that, however, does not cause a quantitative change to housing land in stock. It should also be noted that a part of these plots shift into the rental market, with rental apartment house on them, built as in the case of newly developed land.

Statistics of Housing Land Supply

If the quantitative flow through the distribution routes at each market, as drawn in Figure 3.1., is accurately determinable, we would be able to measure the quantitative supply at each market, either the untapped land market, the newly developed housing land market, or the pre-existing land market. However, the available statistics on housing land do not conform with these definitions, so that secondary statistical references are needed.

Among such secondary statistics are those based on housing land transactions. Any person who has acquired land either in private or corporate capacity is legally required to pay the relevant real estate acquisition tax, which makes it possible for one to determine the size of housing land transactions by selectively using the statistics on such transactions from the available tax statistics (see Table 3.1.). The given figures cover every category from (1) to (8) in Figure 3.1.

According to this table, there are annually around 2.5 million transactions over 5,000 hectares each for housing land supply. These transactions are not limited to within the UPA, but most of the transactions

Table 3.1.
The Number of Cases and Acreage Coming under the Real Estate Acquisition Tax on Housing Land in the Tokyo Region

	Number of cases (1000)	Hectares	Sq m per case
1972		4,935	
1973	282	7,102	251
1974	248	4,751	192
1975	253	5,793	229
1976	252	4,088	162
1977	268	4,482	167
1978	281	4,625	165

Source: National Land Agency, *Kokudo Riyō Hakusho* (White Paper on National Land), various issues.

fall within the UPA. The percentile ratio of 5,000 hectares to the total acreage of the UPA is 320,000 hectares, and the percentile ratio is 1.6 percent; therefore, around 2 percent per year of the total acreage of the UPA is probably subject to housing land transactions. Included in these figures are the cases of switchover of the owners of newly developed housing land ((6), (7), and (8) in Figure 3.1.) as well as multiple transactions on the same land plot within one year. Though these figures cannot exactly represent the physical extent of housing land, they can be used as a kind of yardstick for the maximum of newly developed housing land supply.

Let us now analyze housing land supply in relation to the stock of housing land. Table 3.2. shows the annual transactions of housing land acreage on the basis of the prefectural register of municipal real property taxation. As this table shows, except for the peak at around 8,000 hectares a year from 1971 to 1972, the annual increase in the stock of housing land has been around 5,000 hectares (about 2 percent of the acreage of UPA). However, the actual housing land stock increase should have been less, since the given figures include such business-use land as industrial sites and commercial service installation plots. In addition, the figures include the increase in housing land stock in the area of the rental land and house market.

Apart from the tax-based statistics, the Ministry of Construction publishes the annual "Survey Report on the Acreage of Completed Housing Land Developments" based on information collected from construction businesses about their housing land development projects (see Table 3.3.). These statistics cover close to the total of (3), (4), and (5) plus (9) in Figure 3.1. According to the survey report, the acreage of newly completed housing land was 3,000 to 3,500 hectares annually from

Table 3.2.
Residential Land Area
(*Hectares of taxable real estate*)

	1968	1969	1970	1971	1972	1973	1974	1975	1976
Tokyo	42,400	42,900	43,300	45,000	46,500	46,800	47,900	48,200	48,900
Chiba	29,300	31,100	32,200	33,900	36,400	38,700	40,800	42,600	44,100
Saitama	29,800	31,200	33,100	35,200	37,000	38,700	40,600	42,300	43,600
Kanagawa	32,000	33,700	35,200	37,200	39,400	41,000	42,200	43,600	44,500
Total	133,500	138,900	143,800	151,300	159,300	165,200	171,500	176,700	181,100
Increase over previous year	—	5,400	4,900	7,500	8,000	5,900	6,300	5,200	4,400

Source: Ministry of Home Affairs, *Survey of Real Estate Prices*, annual editions.

Table 3.3.
Area Developed for Residential Use
(*in sq km*)

Prefectures	1969	1970	1971	1972	1973	1974	1975	1976	1977
Tokyo	6.1	6.1	2.4	5.1	3.2	3.6	1.8	2.2	2.2
Chiba	6.3	10.1	13.2	9.5	12.4	10.7	6.9	9.7	8.0
Saitama	2.7	4.1	5.9	6.0	5.8	2.5	3.2	2.2	3.4
Kanagawa	8.3	10.5	12.1	10.4	14.9	5.4	5.8	6.9	5.8
Total	22.0	30.9	34.5	30.5	36.3	22.2	16.7	21.1	18.3

1970 to 1973 but declined to around 2,000 hectares annually beginning in 1974. These figures are, however, too large for those of newly developed housing land supply, since they include newly developed lands for rental housing construction and plots for commercial use.

Table 3.4. shows statistics arranged by the Real Estate Trade Association, which is a trade organization of large real estate dealers. These figures range over (3) and (4) in Figure 3.1. but are conceivably less than the actual transactions in the market, since they do not cover transactions by minor dealers who are not association members. The figures do not include the housing lands developed by the Land Readjustment Associations (discussed in detail later). With replotting of land for readjustment, the Land Readjustment Associations' lots become subject to the ownership of association members who can thereafter be entitled to sell their own lots whenever they choose, which leaves no reliable statistics on their sales each year. However, the actual sale of replotted lots in a year is normally less than one-tenth of the total acreage. Therefore, for this study the acreage of replotted lots is regarded as a new supply to the developed housing land market, and the acreage is figured from the Ministry of Construction materials.

Assuming that Table 3.4. roughly represents the size of the developed housing land market, it can be said that the annual supply of newly developed housing land peaked in 1971 and 1972 and recently started declining to below the 1,000 hectares level, which is equivalent to accommodating only 150,000 persons (based on an average housing plot per household of 200 sq m and an average household size of three persons).

No available statistics can directly show the supply of acreage on the untapped land market. However, the "Survey of Actual Transfer of Farmland" by the Ministry of Agriculture, Forestry, and Fishery offers the approximate acreage of farmland conversion into housing land in the UPA in the Tokyo Region, as shown in Table 3.5. The given figures cover the distribution routes (1) and (2) as well as (5) and (9) in Figure 3.1. Even if all the convertible lands had been part of the untapped

Table 3.4.

Housing Land Developments by Developer Type

(*Hectares*)

		1970	1971	1972	1973	1974	1975	1976	1977	1978
Tokyo	a[1]	240.7	169.7	164.0	87.6	66.2	57.2	78.3	64.4	57.1
	b[2]	155.3	86.7	155.8	207.4	88.6	54.8	91.3	104.9	66.7
	c[3]				210	0	0	140	10	45
Chiba	a	147.0	197.9	162.9	142.5	79.1	71.5	74.5	55.5	90.6
	b	364.1	378.5	457.1	245.7	274.5	136.8	54.2	84.9	76.5
	c				420	280	260	60	340	92
Saitama	a	192.6	208.3	131.9	78.8	31.2	64.6	48.5	20.9	34.5
	b	222.3	454.2	139.8	182.8	155.7	141.3	102.7	46.7	48.4
	c				260	430	250	470	330	27
Kanagawa	a	111.2	131.0	96.7	121.8	50.5	51.6	63.2	45.6	74.2
	b	325.4	583.3	631.7	423.7	412.1	332.7	331.2	206.5	126.6
	c				10	50	130	190	70	104
Total	a	691.5	706.9	555.5	430.7	227.0	244.9	264.5	186.4	256.4
	b	1,067.1	1,502.7	1,384.4	1,059.6	930.9	665.6	579.4	443.0	318.2
	c				900	760	640	860	750	268
Total	a+b+c	1,758.6	2,209.6	1,939.9	2,390	1,918	1,551	1,704	1,379	843
	a+b				1,490.3	1,157.9	910.5	843.9	629.4	574.6

Sources: The Real Estate Trade Association, Survey of Housing Land Supply in the National Capital Region, annual issues, and Ministry of Construction.

[1] Public developers

[2] Private developers

[3] Land readjustment associations

Table 3.5.
Hectares of Farmland Converted to Housing Land in the Urbanization Promotion Areas in the National Capital Region

Year	Hectares converted
1973	3,719
1974	2,200
1975	2,185
1976	2,014
1977	1,936
1978	1,919

Source: National Land Agency, *Kokudo Riyō Hakusho* (White Paper on National Land), annual editions based on Ministry of Agriculture, Forestry, and Fisheries, *Survey on Farmland Transfers.*

land market, the total annual supply of untapped land would be around 2,000 hectares, thus suggesting that the limited acreage of untapped land supply is acting as a constraint on the supply of developed housing land.

The level of housing land supply can well be said in principle to equal the level of housing land demand, since unpurchased land can be called unsold land. In this sense, it can be said that housing land supply was not necessarily insufficient to meet demand. It should be noted that housing land supply was not sufficient as compared with needed land. Supposing that about 1.2 million housing-poor households in the Tokyo Region live under substandard housing conditions, as described earlier. They need 24,000 hectares of housing land on the basis of an average of 200 sq m of housing land per household. The actual annual increase in the housing land stock or in the supply of newly developed housing land is less than one-tenth of their need. If a large majority of them begin negotiations to purchase housing land, the land prices would immediately begin spiraling upward.

Quantitative Demand for Housing Land

Let us now analyze the demand side. Table 3.6. shows the transition of the population of Tokyo metropolis.

The annual transition of the population in Tokyo is relatively stable, though both the efflux and influx are gradually decreasing: About 600,000 persons move in annually, and around the same number of persons flow out.

Table 3.7. shows how the movement of population into and out of the central part of Tokyo, mainly the twenty-three wards, affects the suburban cities and counties in Tokyo metropolis, and the three adjacent

Table 3.6.
Population Movements in the Metropolis of Tokyo

	Total movements	Net increase	Interprefectural movements		Movements within Tokyo
			In	*Out*	
1962	1,882,903	113,357	670,924	557,567	654,412
1963	1,986,333	94,163	687,226	593,063	706,044
1964	2,049,646	34,880	689,503	654,623	705,520
1965	2,097,592	33,121	703,747	670,626	723,219
1966	2,100,316	11,335	700,172	688,837	711,307
1967	2,065,563	− 20,648	682,510	703,158	679,895
1968	2,111,810	− 43,930	696,221	740,151	675,438
1969	2,091,729	− 67,456	680,411	747,867	663,451
1970	2,093,370	− 100,142	668,483	768,625	656,262
1971	2,106,420	− 91,200	668,594	759,794	678,032
1972	2,080,208	− 121,081	649,026	770,107	661,075
1973	2,050,878	− 166,029	627,156	793,185	630,537
1974	1,839,798	− 155,839	565,001	720,840	553,957
1975	1,727,639	− 125,956	541,685	667,641	518,313
1976	1,715,746	− 125,229	529,407	654,636	531,703

Source: Tokyo Metropolitan Government, *Report on Population Movements in the Metropolis of Tokyo* (1978).

prefectures. As this table shows, around 400,000 people annually flow into the central part of Tokyo from its peripheral areas, while about the same amount of population flows therefrom into these areas. The reasons for this population influx into the central part of Tokyo include occupational requirements (70 percent), schooling requirements (20 percent), and marriage (10 percent). Of the occupational-linked moves, about half are for employment transfer within the same organizations, while the rest are for new employment, thus indicating that the population influx into the central part of Tokyo basically consists of people in relatively young age brackets who throng into large cities for jobs and educational opportunities. On the other hand, the reasons for the population efflux from the central part of Tokyo into its peripheral areas are housing requirements (60 percent), environmental requirements (10 percent), marriage requirements (10 percent), occupational requirements (10 percent), and others (10 percent). In other words, those who move out of the central part of Tokyo do so for housing requirements. In reality, about 80 percent of the outflowing population (including the 10 percent each for environmental and marriage requirements) consist of those who move out of the central part of Tokyo for housing reasons. This 80 percent dominates housing demand in the vicinities of Tokyo.

Table 3.7.
Population Movements into and out of the Metropolitan Center
of Tokyo (Twenty-three Wards)

| | | Out of | Into | Net |
	Years	Tokyo center (in 1000)		change
Total	1966	623	670	−47
	1976	541	695	−154
A[1]	1966	400	231	169
	1976	322	288	34
B[2]	1966	223	439	−216
	1976	219	407	−188

Source: Ibid.
[1]Prefectures other than B.
[2]Chiba, Saitama, and Kanagawa plus Tokyo outside of the twenty-three Wards.

Suppose that 400,000 persons annually move from the central part of Tokyo into the peripheral areas, and 80 percent of them, forming a standard three-person household, need houses. A total of about 110,000 houses are needed for them per year, thus giving rise to demand for 2,200 hectares of housing land on the basis of an average of 200 sq m of housing plot per household. This demand was equivalent to the supply of newly developed housing land back in 1971 and 1972, suggesting that demand and supply were balanced based on the newly developed housing land market in that period. However, along with the decline of newly developed housing land supply thereafter, the average size of housing plots per household has inevitably become smaller.

Section 2. The Behavior Patterns of Untapped Landowners

Fact-Finding Study of Farmer Households

Prior to the designation of UPAs, the owners of farmlands and woodlands had largely been farmers. In the process of housing land development, they must have either sold such lands or developed these into housing land by themselves (see Figure 3.1.). In other words, the owners of farmlands and woodlands played an important role in the process of conversion of such lands into housing lands. Therefore, it is essential to analyze the behavior patterns of such landowners.

Based on the research assistance aid from National Institute for Research Advancement, I recently conducted a detailed interview-based survey with about 400 farmer households that had land in UPAs in the National Capital Sphere. Though the questionnaire covered many personal questions such as household income, retained property, and land sales, I believe that the survey returns are reliable. Before giving the results, let me summarize the main features of the eight survey areas in four cities. These surveys were conducted in Matsudo and Abiko in August and September 1978 and in Machida and Kawasaki in December 1979.

Kanamori Area in Machida City. This area is within ten to fifteen minutes on foot from the Machida Station, one of the express stops of the Odakyu Line (a private railway running southwestwards from Shinjuku), where urbanization has progressed notably since 1960. It has a large number of farmer-owned rental houses and apartment houses, and farmland plots still co-exist with residential housing plots.

Naruse Area in Machida City. This area is farther away than the Kanamori Area from the Machida Station and rather closer to the Suzukakedai and the Tsukushino Stations of the Denen-Toshi Line (a private railway running from Shibuya through the southern suburbs of Tokyo). As compared with the Kanamori Area, its history of urbanization is shorter. However, large-scale land readjustment was advanced under the initiative of the local agricultural cooperative association, and it forms a typical suburban housing quarter.

Chiyogaok/Manpukuji/Ozenji Area in Kawasaki City. This area is about twenty minutes on foot from the Yurigaoka Station of the Odakyu Line, which is closer to the urban center of Tokyo than the Machida Station. The station was opened in 1960 following the Japan Housing Corporation's development of a large housing complex, and the progress of housing development in this area lags behind Machida City. In addition to a land readjustment project arranged by the Japan Housing Corporation, it has large-scale housing developments by private corporations. Farmland and woodlands, however, also notably remain scattered throughout this area.

Hosoyama/Kanehodo/Yamaguchi Area in Kawasaki City. As this area is located outside the Chiyogaoka/Manpukuji/Ozenji Area, its urbanization lags behind accordingly. The Shin-Yurigaoka Station of the Odakyu Line in nearly the center of the Yamaguchi Area was opened in 1976 to meet the need of the Tama New Town. A large-scale land readjustment project is currently under way there.

Sakae-machi Area in Matsudo City. Since this area is a few hundred meters west of the Matsudo Station of the Joban Line (of the Japan National Railways Corporation), it already has single- or two-story houses built together in a congested manner with a large number of farmer-owned rental houses and apartment houses and with farmland scattered among the houses.

Koda/Koganehara Area in Matsudo City. This area spreads the northwest of the Shin-Matsudo Station, which is the next to the Matsudo Station of the Joban Line, where large-scale land readjustment projects were begun by the Japan Housing Corporation and the Matsudo Municipality since 1963. These projects already are completed, and the construction there of medium- and high-rise condominium housing buildings is currently under way.

Koyadai/Sageto Area in Abiko City. This area is a few hundred meters south of the Tennodai Station, which is farther away than the Matsudo or the Shin-Matsudo Station of the Joban Line. A land readjustment project already is completed in the area, and the construction of single- and two-story houses is going on.

Shibazaki Area in Abiko City. This area is a few hundred meters north of the Tennodai Station of the Joban Line. Though land readjustment has started in a part of this area, the area as a whole still retains the character of a farm village, with one part designated as the Urbanization Control Area (UCA). Though the sites around farm houses have been designated as a UPA, their farm plots are left intact within the UCA, and the urbanization of this area has not progressed rapidly.

Size of Farmer Household

As Table 3.8. shows in a by-size breakdown of the number of farmers in these four cities, farmers who operate on farm acreage of 0.5 hectare or more but less than 1 hectare comprise the largest group and make up one-quarter of the total. Next come those who operate on 1 hectare or more but less than 1.5 hectares and those on 0.3 hectare or more but less than 0.5 hectare. As compared with Machida and Kawasaki, farm sizes are relatively larger in Matsudo and Abiko, and this is especially true of the Shibazaki Area. It should be added in this connection that a comparison of the distribution of farm-size groups in the survey areas and the results of the Agriculture Census in the Southern Kanto Region (where all the survey areas are included) showed a similar pattern, thus indicating that the samples well represented the whole.

In the aspect of agricultural income, the largest number of farmer households are in the bracket of less than Yen 1 million of agricultural turnover a year. In other words, an overwhelming majority of farmer households cannot live on agricultural income alone. The agricultural incomes of farmer households in Matsudo and Abiko are larger than those in Machida and Kawasaki. Large farm income households are

Table 3.8.
Number of Farmer Households by Size of Farm Land Owned

Target Area	Machida		Kawasaki		Matsudo		Abiko		Machida and Kawasaki	Matsudo and Abiko	Total	(%)
Class	Kanomori	Naruse	Hosoyama	Chiyogaoka	Sakaemachi	Koda	Shibasaki	Koyadai				
–0.1 ha	13	19	9	17	2	0	0	0	58	2	60	(15.0)
0.1–0.3	7	16	14	23	6	2	0	2	60	10	70	(17.5)
0.3–0.5	7	3	8	10	3	5	2	2	28	12	40	(10.0)
0.5–1.0	8	16	10	10	17	15	13	14	44	59	103	(25.7)
1.0–1.5	1	—	2	1	16	18	12	18	4	64	68	(17.0)
1.5–2.0	1	—	—	3	2	8	11	7	4	28	32	(8.0)
2.0–3.0	—	—	—	—	4	2	10	7	—	23	23	(5.7)
3.0–	1	—	—	—	—	—	2	—	1	2	3	(0.7)
No answer	1	—	1	—	—	—	—	—	2	—	2	(0.5)
Total	39	54	44	64	50	50	50	50	201	200	401	(100.0)

found more often in Koda, Koganehara, and Shibazaki than in other areas.

As is apparent from the above, Matsudo and Abiko rely more on agriculture than Machida and Kawasaki. Machida and Kawasaki also have been more affected by urbanization, while Matsudo and Abiko have always leaned more strongly to agriculture. However, in terms of the total income of the farmer household, with nonagricultural income added to agricultural income, the farmer households in Machida and Kawasaki are better off than those in Matsudo and Abiko (see Table 3.9.).

Though the farmer households in the income bracket ranging over Yen 2 million or more but not exceeding Yen 4 million a year comprise a majority, there are also farmer households in the bracket upward from Yen 4 million to Yen 6 million and the bracket from Yen 6 million upward to Yen 10 million. In the case of urban worker households, the ceilings of the second and the fourth of five total income brackets were, respectively, around Yen 2 million and Yen 4 million; the farmer households in the sample areas can generally be called rich. It should be noted in particular that most of the farmer households in Kanamori, Naruse, and Sakae-machi have annual incomes equivalent to the richest fifth of urban worker households.

What makes this group rich is nonagricultural income. Around one-third of them have nonagricultural incomes from Yen 2 million to Yen 4 million, thus earning more from nonagricultural sources than from agriculture.

Table 3.10. shows a categorical breakdown of nonagricultural income sources of farmers; rental houses and apartment houses are the most common income sources for them. With other types of real estate leasing added to housing rental services, real esate leasing consists of one-half of the identified categories of nonagricultural income sources for part-time farmer households or one-quarter of those for both the part-time and the full-time farmer households as a whole. In Sakae-machi, all the part-time farmer households and 80 percent of all the farmer households engage in real estate leasing. Among the other categories of income sources, white-collar and store managers respectively hold notable shares. Though housing rental service is predominant among farmers in Kanamori, Sakae-machi, Koda, Koganehara, Koyadai, and Sageto, white-collar and store managers are larger shares in the other areas.

Real estate leasing yields notably significant returns from Yen 2 million upward to Yen 4 million. However, some farmers earn leasing income of over Yen 10 million a year. Real estate leasing has become the most reliable income source for farmer households. Two-thirds of farmers who lease real estates have incomes therefrom derive more than 40 percent of their total income from this source.

Table 3.9.
Number of Farmer Households by Household Income

Target Area	Machida		Kawasaki		Matsudo		Abiko		Machida and Kawasaki	Matsudo and Abiko	Total	(%)
Class	Kanomori	Naruse	Hosoyama	Chiyogaoka	Sakaemachi	Koda	Shibasaki	Koyadai				
−2 million yen	1	1	2	4	—	1	—	—	8	1	9	(2.2)
2–4	10	12	16	16	9	22	29	22	54	82	136	(33.9)
4–6	8	12	17	22	14	15	16	15	59	60	119	(29.7)
6–8	14	17	6	13	16	9	3	10	50	38	} 97	(24.2)
8–10	} 3	} 6	} 2	} 2	4	3	—	} 2	} 13	9		
10–12					2	—	—			2		
12–15	} 3	} 6	} 2	} 7	5	—	2	} 1	} 17	} 8	} 40	(10.0)
15–			1		—	—	—					
Total	39	54	44	64	50	50	50	50	201	200	401	(100.0)

Table 3.10.
Number of Farmer Households by Type of Secondary Occupation

Target Area / Type	Machida		Kawasaki		Matsudo		Abiko		Machida and Kawasaki	Matsudo and Abiko	Total (%)
	Kanomori	Naruse	Hosoyama	Chiyogaoka	Sakaemachi	Koda	Shibasaki	Koyadai			
Rent house or room	9	9	5	4	33	13	2	12	27	60	87 (40.1)
Small shop owner	4	5	5	14	—	4	4	7	28	15	43 (19.8)
White-collar worker	3	13	16	19	—	4	2	1	51	7	58 (26.7)
Blue-collar worker	2	7	—	2	—	5	—	1	11	6	17 (7.8)
Rent parking lot	—	—	—	—	2	—	1	—	—	3	3 (1.4)
Miscellaneous	0	0	2	0	6	0	1	0	2	7	9 (4.2)
Total	18	34	28	39	41	26	10	21	119	98	217 (100.0)

One way to determine when farmers started such real estate leasing is to check the annual construction starts of rental houses and apartment houses. The building of rental houses started early in Machida—even before 1960—and achieved its peak in 1969 to 1970. Kawasaki and Matsudo followed Machida, and Abiko lagged behind them. The building of rental apartment houses generally started after the building of rental houses, and its peak came after 1969 in Machida and Kawasaki. The building of such apartment houses became notable in Matsudo around 1973 but is still insignificant in Abiko. Most of owned houses of the farmer households were built after 1960.

Retained Assets of Farmer Households

In analyzing the situation of farmers' retained assets I will begin with woodland and will exclude farmland, which was described above. Two-thirds of farmer households in the sample areas possess no woodland at all. With the owners of woodland less than 1 hectare included, only 10 percent of them have woodland to a significant level. There are comparatively larger woodland owners in the Chiyogaoka/Manpukuji/Ozenji and the Koyadai/Sageto areas.

Households that have their own housing plots (from 600 sq m upward to 1,000 sq m) are the largest group. Then come those that have plots from 1,000 sq m upward to 1,500 sq m. Their housing plots are reasonable for farmer households though may appear large by the standard of midtown housing space.

Around one-half of farmer households own housing land other than their own housing plots, and the number of such farmer households is larger than the number of those that earn income from real estate leases.

As Table 3.11. shows, the largest group of farmer households own from 1 to 2 hectares of land, and farmers in Matsudo and Abiko have comparatively larger amounts of land than those in Machida and Kawasaki. One-half of farmers estimated their real estate at above Yen 100 million for each household. More of the richer farmer households reside in more urbanized Sakae-machi and Kanamori. On the other hand, less than 20 percent of farmers estimated their real estate at below Yen 50 million for each household. The amounts estimated were by farmers themselves, and if their real estate were estimated at market value, the estimates would obviously increase by several times because farmers tend to underestimate their assets for fear of incurring a heavier tax.

On the other hand, farmers who were asked about liquid assets answered mostly that they held assets below Yen 10 million, thus indi-

Table 3.11.
Number of Farmer Households by Size of Land Owned

Target Area	Machida		Kawasaki		Matsudo		Abiko		Machida and Kawasaki	Matsudo and Abiko	Total (%)
Class	Kanomori	Naruse	Hosoyama	Chiyogaoka	Sakaemachi	Koda	Shibasaki	Koyadai			
–0.1 ha	2	4	1	4	—	—	—	—	11	—	11 (2.7)
0.1–0.3	9	13	9	17	2	1	—	—	48	3	51 (12.7)
0.3–0.5	5	9	13	14	5	3	1	1	41	10	51 (12.7)
0.5–1.0	12	17	8	14	18	13	9	11	51	51	102 (25.4)
1.0–2.0	5	7	8	7	20	27	25	23	27	95	122 (30.4)
2.0–3.0	2	2	4	3	5	6	9	9	11	29	40 (10.0)
3.0–5.0	2	2	—	1	—	—	6	6	5	12	22 (5.5)
5.0–	1	—	—	4	—	—			5		
No Answer	1	—	1	—	—	—	—	—	2	—	2 (0.5)
Total	39	54	44	64	50	50	50	50	201	200	401 (100.0)

cating that the retained deposits, savings, bonds, debentures, and company stocks for each household is far less than their estimated retained real estate. Regarding the relationship of estimated amount of real estate in one's possession and annual income, larger real estate holders tended to have higher annual incomes. However, their individual annual incomes are not large at all compared with the estimated amounts of their retained real estate. Seventy-three of the farmer households holding real estate of less than Yen 100 million and only six of those holding real estates exceeding Yen 100 million were found to earn annual incomes exceeding 10 percent of estimated real estates. Generally, the income ratio against the estimated real estates is lower in Matsudo and Abiko than in Machida and Kawasaki.

Farmers' Land Sale Behavior

Farmers' land sale behavior is significant because such lands compose most of the supply of land for housing. Nearly all of the farmer households sold land at least once in the past (see Table 3.12.). Around one-third of them sold land for two times or more, but only fifteen of them sold land for five times or more.

The total acreage of land sold by individual farmer households ranged from less than 300 sq m to over 6,000 sq m. However, the acreage of sold land was far less than what was expected. Two-thirds of all the interviewed farmer households sold less than 20 percent of their initially owned acreage. There were none at all in Matsudo and Abiko who sold more than 60 percent of initially owned acreage, and in Machida and Kawasaki twenty-three, or only 10 percent of the total, fell in this category (see Table 3.13.). The fact that Machida and Kawasaki are ahead of Matsudo and Abiko in this aspect of land sale probably is further evidence that the former is more urbanized. In the case of Matsudo and Abiko, farmers sold an average 15 percent of their initially owned lands in thirteen years—around 1 percent a year. The farmers interviewed actually were engaged in agriculture at that time; in other words, those who discontinued farming were automatically excluded. However, as is discernible from the limited number of those interviewed who sold more than 60 percent of their initially owned lands, the number of farmers excluded from the survey must have been insignificant.

The amount of income from land sales is also not as large as generally has been thought. The cases of more than Yen 100 million in payment from land sales are less than 10 percent of the total.

Among the areas of the survey were those where land readjustment projects were ongoing. In the Koganehara area, for instance, the land sales in the readjustment zone by twenty-eight farmer households each

Table 3.12.
Number of Farmer Households by Number of Times of Land Disposal

Target Area / Class	Machida		Kawasaki		Matsudo		Abiko		Machida and Kawasaki	Matsudo and Abiko	Total (%)	
	Kanomori	Naruse	Hosoyama	Chiyogaoka	Sakaemachi	Koda	Shibasaki	Koyadai				
0	8	5	11	9	3	18	11	5	33	37	70	(17.5)
1	12	19	20	31	20	20	24	20	82	84	166	(41.4)
2	9	13	4	8	18	7	12	18	34	55	89	(22.2)
3	5	6	3	3	6	5	—	6	17	17	34	(8.5)
4	2	4	1	1	1	—	—	1	8	2	10	(2.5)
5	1	4	2	1	1	—	—	—	8	1	9	(2.2)
6	—	1	—	1	—	—	—	—	2	—	2	(0.5)
7	1	—	—	1	—	—	—	—	2	—	2	(0.5)
More than 8	1	—	—	1	1	—	—	—	2	—	2	(0.5)
No Answer	—	2	3	8	1	—	3	—	13	4	17	(4.2)
Total	39	54	44	64	50	50	50	50	201	200	401	(100.0)

Table 3.13.
Proportions of Disposed Land to Owned Land
(Eight Target Areas Total)

$\dfrac{B}{A}$ A	0 %	0–10 %	10–20 %	20–30 %	30–40 %	40–50 %	50–60 %
−0.3 ha	20	2	2	2	3	1	3
0.3–0.5	14	5	2	2	6	3	2
0.5–1.0	18	18	19	15	9	5	5
1.0–2.0	24	38	31	21	9	6	5
2.0–3.0	6	25	14	8	6	0	1
3.0–	4	11	6	2	0	2	1
Total	86	99	74	50	33	17	17

A = Area of Land Owned in 1965
B = Area of Land Disposed since 1966

holding more than 2,000 sq m of land in the area again indicated that the actual land sales had been less than generally thought. During the period from the land replotting in 1971 to the 1978 survey year, one-quarter of them had sold no land therein at all, and the actually sold land acreage in the seven years was 12 percent, or an average of only 2 percent a year. Consequently, there still are many vacant housing plots in the project zone, even though the alleged purpose of the land readjustment was to supply good-quality housing land. From 1971 to 1978, housing plots increased from 117 to 292. This increase was mainly attributable to the fragmentation of initial plots; the actual increase was around 3 hectares in housing-occupied acreage (from around 13 hectares to around 16 hectares), which accounted for only a 12 percent increase as compared with the total acreage of around 22 hectares for the project zone. In other words, compared to around 9 hectares of vacant housing land plots that were there as of 1971, the actual increase of housing land supply—that is, the housing land plots where houses have been built, including apartment houses, by either the plot purchasers or landowners—was 31 percent (or approximately 5 percent a year). This indicates the slow growth of housing land supply, since better conditions exist in a land readjustment project zone than in general farmland areas for expediting land sales, since landowners have already agreed with one another to convert their lands into housing use prior to the start of the project.

Farmers' Motive for Land Sale

The causes of such slow progress in land sales can be determined by analyzing the landowners' motives for land sale. Table 3.14. shows how turnovers from land sales have been spent. According to the breakdown of how profits were spent, the highest percentage went for savings, deposits, and investment in stocks; the second went for rebuilding personal dwellings; the third for building rental houses and apartment houses; the fourth for alternative land purchases; and the fifth for payment of the inheritance tax. The category of "Others" covers amounts spent purchasing goods.

According to the breakdown of the amount of money spent for the listed purposes, the highest percentages are for saving and investment and for inheritance tax payment purposes. Next comes spending for building rental and apartment houses, for rebuilding personal dwellings, and for alternative land purchases. The percentage of money spent for building rental and apartment houses and for rebuilding personal dwellings is higher in Matsudo and Abiko than in Machida and Kawasaki. One reason for this can be that land prices were relatively low when the farmers sold their land in these two cities.

In searching for the motive for farmers' saving deposits and investment in stock, I reviewed all such cases and found that in only 22 cases out of 277 was all the turnover from land sale spent for this purpose. However, in almost all other cases a large portion of the turnover from the land sale was spent for other categories such as paying the inheritance tax, building rental houses, or rebuilding their own houses, and

Table 3.14.
Reasons for Land Disposal

Reasons	Number of cases	Gross sale	Average gross sale per case
Living expenses	32	412[1]	13[1]
Building owned house	157	5,903	38
Education or marriage of children	24	280	12
Inheritance tax	81	12,612	156
Building house or apartments for rent	134	8,388	63
Purchase of land	93	2,790	30
Investment for private concern	11	728	66
Investment for stock, bond, and saving	256	6,144	24
Miscellaneous	148	6,822	46
Total	938	44,079	47

[1]Thousands of yens

the remaining money was transformed into deposit, bonds, and stocks. The category of saving and investment is therefore supplementary to other motives, even though it is more frequent. Here it should be noted that eleven cases out of twenty-two cases in which all the profits from the land sale were spent for saving and investment were found in the less-urbanized Chiyogaoka/Manpukuji/Ozenji area, where an estate dealer bought a good amount of woodland from farmers very recently. But farmers there are still engaged in farming and feel that the demand for rental houses is not strong; therefore all the money is transformed into bonds and stocks as a stopgap.

The category of greatest amount of money spent for the listed purposes per case is the inheritance tax payment, followed by the spending for building rental houses, and the spending for rebuilding personal dwellings.

To sum up, the motives of farmers for selling land can largely be categorized as the need for rebuilding their own houses, for building rental houses and apartment houses, and for paying the inheritance tax, with the needs for alternative land purchases and for investments in saving, deposits, and stocks as supplementary motives.

Regionally, the percentage of land sales for the purpose of building rental houses and apartment houses is high in the heavily urbanized Kanamori and Sakae-machi areas, while land sales for the purpose of inheritance tax payments are notable in the least-urbanized Shibazaki area. The rebuilding of personal dwellings is a common practice in all sampled areas.

The data suggest that as soon as these purposes are fulfilled, farmers become reluctant to sell their lands. In order for this point to be confirmed, farmers who had built their own houses and/or rental houses in the preceding twenty years were asked about their future plans for building such houses. Their answers were negative with regard to their own houses, and many of those who already had rental houses had no plans to build more rental houses.

Land Sale Over Time

Land sales started relatively earlier in Machida and Kawasaki and marked the first peak around 1960. The first peak in land sales in Matsudo and Abiko came as late as in 1967. Behind this time difference lay the difference in when the tide of urbanization arrived in each area. What was common between the two areas was that the land sales climaxed from 1967 to 1975.

It should be noted in Table 3.15., which shows annual land sales from 1965 to 1977, that land sales suddenly increased from 1969 to 1970

Table 3.15.
Land Sales by Year

Year	Number of cases		Acreage (ha)		Turnover (million yen)		Unit price (thousand yen/sq m)		Average size per case (hundred sq m)		Average turnover per case (million yen)	
	Machida and Kawasaki	Matsudo and Abiko	Machida and Kawasaki	Matsudo and Abiko	Machida and Kawasaki	Matsudo and Abiko	Machida and Kawasaki	Matsudo and Abiko	Machida and Kawasaki	Matsudo and Abiko	Machida and Kawasaki	Matsudo and Abiko
1965	18	12	8.33	1.50	668	54	80	36	46	12	37	5
1966	11	4	1.27	0.54	99	30	78	56	12	14	9	8
1967	24	25	5.36	6.23	487	119	91	19	22	25	20	5
1968	8	28	2.05	5.29	119	289	58	55	25	19	15	10
1969	11	11	1.58	1.74	125	94	79	54	14	17	11	9
1970	26	33	8.22	4.15	901	492	110	119	32	13	35	15
1971	16	21	2.72	2.25	364	334	134	148	17	11	22	16
1972	20	21	4.38	2.93	990	616	226	210	21	14	49	29
1973	14	23	2.05	2.54	673	495	328	195	15	11	49	22
1974	11	21	2.02	3.60	402	1176	199	326	18	17	37	55
1975	21	19	3.61	1.37	2070	452	573	329	17	7	99	33
1976	11	10	0.40	0.71	254	272	635	383	4	7	23	27
1977	18	15	0.58	0.99	400	345	689	348	3	7	22	23

and declined remarkably from 1975 to 1976, which coincide with the years when substantial revisions were made in the capital gains tax system. In 1970 this system was changed from progressive rate taxation on aggregate income to proportional rate taxation on separated land sales income in order to reduce tax on the gains from land sale. In 1976 the progressive rate taxation on aggregate income was revived in place of the proportional rate taxation on separated land sales income in order to increase tax on such gains. There is no doubt that land sales expanded while the tax reduction was in effect and declined thereafter. What is more, since any downward revision in taxation was usually preceded by public discussion of the appropriateness of its implementation, such discussion may conceivably have led landowners to carry planned land sales over to years when they could expect more benefits from the tax reduction. (See the more detailed discussion of the tax system below.)

Regarding changes in acreage of sold land, amount of income, and unit land prices, there is a tendency for less acreage to be sold but for unit land prices to rise. Though income per sale tends to rise, its upturn is far more moderate than the rise of unit land price.

Prospect for Land Sales by Farmers

Among the 401 interviewed farmer households, only 71 are positive about possible land sales in the next ten years. In Machida and Kawasaki, where more land sales were registered to date, fewer farmer households (21) were positive in this respect than in Matsudo and Abiko. The motives for intended land sales are largely building rental houses and apartment houses, paying inheritance tax payments, and expanding or rebuilding personal dwellings. Though a sizable share of actual land sales were invested in saving deposit accounts and/or stocks, only one household referred to this motive. Regarding the size of future land sales, approximately two-thirds of them in both urbanizing areas think "very small." The relatively low-income farmer households are more positive about their possibility of future land sales.

One interview question asked farmers about future land prices. Two-thirds of them expect continuing land price rises. Regionally, farmers in Machida and Kawasaki are more optimistic about future land price rises than those in Matsudo and Abiko. A part of this difference might be attributed to the time lag between the surveys; the survey in Machida and Kawasaki was held about one year after the one in Matsudo and Abiko, and in this period the tendency for land prices to rise had generally strengthened. Most of the remaining one-third think that land prices will level off, and only eleven farmers answered that land prices might turn downward.

Regarding their reasons for this perspective, most bullish farmers felt that their lands were convenient for housing locations. A considerable number of them also noted other economic reasons for their optimism, such as the persistent housing land shortage and continued consumer price hikes. On the other hand, their main reasons for predicting that the land prices would level off were that the high price level is already beyond the reach of buyers at large and that the land price boom is already over.

With a view to finding out their expected behaviors in response to future land price transitions, I asked three hypothetical questions: "Would you sell land if the land price rises further?" "Would you sell land if the land price remains the same as the current level?" "Would you sell land if the land price goes down?" Two-thirds of farmers replied with negative answers to all of these questions. I identify them as status quo farmers—those who would not sell under any market trend.

More than 80 percent of farmer households in Machida and Kawasaki and 50 percent in Matsudo and Abiko are status quo farmers. Those who had the intention to sell land on the basis of their either somewhat bearish or bullish prospects for future land price, respectively, comprise one-fifth of farmers in Matsudo and Abiko. Among the farmer households in Matsudo and Abiko are those who still earn a substantial part of their household income from agriculture and are not well satisfied with their income level or living standard, including housing conditions. Though these farmer households give some thought to the possibility of selling land, most farmer households in Machida and Kawasaki have already achieved a satisfactory income level and seem to have no strong motivation for selling land, except for the need to pay the inheritance tax.

These status quo farmers are not necessarily full-time farmers. Generally, their income from nonagricultural sources is larger than their income from agriculture, and their gross income is higher than that of farmers who think about selling land.

Furthermore, many of these status quo farmers have already experienced land sales in the past. Among status quo farmers are certainly those who have never sold land in the past and are still determined to earn a living mainly on agriculture. However, a majority of the farmers of this type consist of those who have stable incomes from rental houses and apartments houses that were built with the gains from land sales and no longer think about selling any more land.

Section 3. Peculiarities of the Land Market

Hypothesis of Target Profit (Amount-Fixed Profit)

Insofar as the behavior of untapped landowners is as was analyzed in the preceding section, the land market where such owners act as untapped land suppliers should have significant peculiarities apart from the market for industrial products. Since the untapped landowners sell land only when they have specific objectives and need the income for achieving those objectives, the profit maximization hypothesis, which is generally accepted in economics as underlying the pattern of corporate behavior, is not applicable to this market, and the target income amounts that the suppliers individually determine play an important role in determining supply. Because most of farmers acquired their farmlands either by virtue of the postwar Agrarian Land Reform or inheritance, their land acquisition costs must have been negligibly small as compared with the current land price level. Thus, their income from land sales can be considered wholly profit. Insofar as the untapped land suppliers act subject to the prescribed pattern of behavior for achieving the target profit, land supply would lessen as land prices move higher, since the supply varies in inverse proportion to the fluctuation of price, provided that the expected profit is fixed at a given level.[2]

However, since an untapped landowner under normal circumstances may sell no land if his expected income from land sale is less than the profit he can gain by using the land for farming, the quantitative supply of untapped land would be zero once its price falls below a certain level.

The end users of housing land are mainly commuters to major cities. They generally want the largest land plots available provided that the land prices are acceptable. The demand curve in a given area therefore can be said to decline rightward. Housing land users usually try to acquire both housing plots and houses within the limit of their funds, thus causing no exact inverse proportion between price and quantity of land. Since direct buyers of untapped land—such as public land developers and private real estate dealers—are expected to act in correspondence with demand on the part of housing land end users, their demand curve also declines rightward.

Suppose that the demand curve is given as DD in Figure 3.2. The supply curve intersects the demand curve at two points—A and B—and A shows the stable equilibrium point. If market price P rises higher than Pa in Figure 3.2. for some reason (P > Pa), the market price would be pressed downward insofar as the suppliers and users are expected to act simultaneously in response to a given price, since quantitative

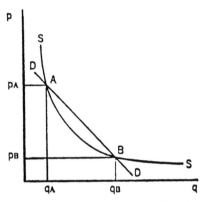

Figure 3.2. *Market model under the hypothesis of fixed amount profit.*

supply exceeds quantitative demand at market price P. If market price P is between Pa and Pb (Pa > P > Pb), the market price would be pressed upward because quantitative demand exceeds quantitative supply. Therefore, Point A becomes the stable equilibrium point when the market price is higher than Pb. If market price P is lower than Pb, the market price would fall, with quantitative supply exceeding quantitative demand and thus turning into the range of farmland or woodland prices.

As long as demand for housing land is weak in a given area, demand falls below the hyperbolic part of the supply curve and closer to the origin, thus bringing the price of untapped land close to the farmland or woodland price level. However, as demand gains strength and starts moving upward as DD in Figure 3.2., the price begins rising rapidly toward Pa with one reason or another as a turning point. In this upturn process, the price rise rate is presumably large.

The prescribed rules are applicable to the initial stage of untapped land transactions, but the market behavior may change at the next stage. Farmers who have attained their target profits after supplying land in the process of land price rise may no longer be tied to the need to sell untapped land, and the supply curve will shift to the southwest. Even if market equilibrium is achieved, once farmers gain their target profits from land sales to the market and lose their motives for land supply, the supply curve would shift closer to the southwestern corner.

Again, the supply curve for untapped land differs from that of general commodities. That is, the supply curve for general commodities is determined apart from the demand curve and is normally stable for some time. However, the supply curve for untapped land tends to shift to a new position whenever a transaction occurs.

The same can also be said about the demand curve. An end user who has acquired housing land leaves the market and will not come back for some time. The demand curve then also seems to shift closer to the southwestern corner. However, on the demand side, there are constantly new demand entries along with the population influx into major cities and the rise of workers' income level, which thus shifts the demand curve northeasternly but seldomly southwesternly. With the preceding equilibrium disrupted, a new equilibrium price surfaces but always on a level higher than the former. Though the price rises, the volume of transaction decreases, thus leaving large farmland and woodland sprawling with housing areas.

The southeastern segment of the demand curve represents demand that has not been met with supply. Then, this demand shifts into another area farther away from midtown. The new area is inconvenient for commuting, but potential users can find therein more untapped land and more potential suppliers who are ready to sell land. In Figure 3.3., S'S' is the supply curve in the inside areas, and SS is that for outside. Since such new areas are larger in acreage than the areas closer to the midtowns and have more farmer households accommodated, SS stays always northeasternly of S'S'.

Since commuters pay more for a space of land in an area closer to midtown than for the same space in an outlying area, DD can be said to represent the demand curve for all commutable areas. The equilibrium price of untapped land inside is always higher than that outside.

Differences between Land and Ordinary Commodities

The figure that shows the supply curve of housing land with a negative slope (i.e., Figure 3.3.) may look odd to readers who have studied economics because in orthodox economics the supply curve shows an upward slope, as in Figure 3.4. It should be recalled here why the

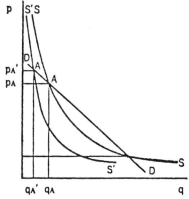

Figure 3.3. *Model of land market.*

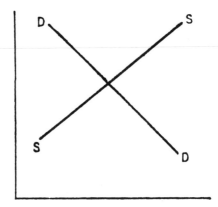

Figure 3.4. *Ordinary market model.*

supply curve slopes upward in the case of ordinary commodities. Samuelson's *Economics* (10th ed. 1976:63), a typical textbook on economics, contains the following paragraph:

> [O]ur old friend the law of diminishing returns provides one strong reason why the supply curve would slope upward. If society wants more wine, then more and more labor will have to be added to the same limited hill sites suitable for producing wine grapes. Even if this industry is too small to affect the general wage rate, each new man will—according to the law of diminishing returns—be adding less and less extra product; and hence the necessary cost to coax out additional product will have to rise.

The law of diminishing returns here means that in successively applying equal amounts of labor for production, an added application yields a lesser increase in production. This alone, however, is insufficient to explain the upward slope of the supply curve because this represents that more supply requires extra unit cost: In other words, it needs progressive marginal cost increases. Given a market price, each supplier can logically produce as much as he or she wishes insofar as production costs stay less than price, though the supplier would not dare to produce if cost becomes higher than price. The ceiling of supply can therefore be determined, but a supply curve cannot. How does a supplier determine supply quantity under a given market price? The decision is said to be made at a point where the market price agrees with marginal cost. In this respect, according to Professor Samuelson (1976:455–456),

> He will do this because he is interested in maximizing the total profit he can earn. Profit is the difference between the total revenue he receives from selling his output and the total cost incurred in producing that output. He increases his total so long as the extra revenue brought in from the last unit sold is greater than the extra cost which that last unit entailed. Total profit

reaches its peak—is maximized—when there is no longer any extra profit to be earned by selling extra output. The last little unit he produces and sells is just in balance as far as extra revenue and extra cost are concerned. What is that extra revenue? It is price per unit. What is that extra cost? It is marginal cost.

In other words, in the case of ordinary economic goods, the supply curve slopes upward because the law of diminishing returns and the principle of profit maximization are generally accepted.

On the other hand, take the case of a farmer in the UPA. The cost of his land acquisition either owing to the Agrarian Land Reform or by inheritance was nearly negligible, and the cost for selling a part of his land or woodland probably consists of the commission to be paid to a real estate broker and the cost for setting aside redundant agricultural machinery and tools; this cost can be said to be virtually proportional to the size of land for sale and is at least not progressive. Though the capital gain tax rate is currently progressive (in this sense, the accompanying tax cost is progressive), it had been proportional during the period from 1970 to 1976, and even now the rate is proportional while the amount of capital gain is within a given limit (less than Yen 40 million a year).

Generally speaking, it is difficult to increase land as an economic resource. In order to increase land supply, land reclamation and landfills are needed. Since the cost for such reclamation and landfills increases as the depth of water over reclaimable land increases, some people claim that land supply is also subject to the law of diminishing returns. However, what is being discussed here is the supply of housing land in the UPAs in the National Capital Sphere and not land in general. With farmland and woodland utilized, the supply of untapped land can be increased (as was prescribed in Section 1 of this chapter).

If a landowner could accurately forecast future land prices for the parts of land he plans to sell in the future, if he could predict the expected satisfaction he may derive from each future land sale, and if he could have a table of reliable discount rate for comparison of current satisfaction with expected future satisfaction (until the time of his death), he might be able to determine the size of land for every phase of future sales. However, such presuppositions are unrealistic. Most untapped landowners are vaguely looking forward to further land price rises, and what they are wary of is a danger of inviting loss because of misleading forecasts. Therefore, the surest way for those who look forward to land price increases to avoid an error is not to sell land—except, for instance, when a certain amount of cash is needed to rebuild their own houses, to build rental apartment houses or rental houses for earning extra income, or to pay the inheritance tax. In other words, what rules here is the postulate of target profit and not the postulate of profit maximization.

In addition to the above, consumers' price rises (inflation) act as another factor that discourages farmers from land sales because even if a farmer purchases, for instance, bonds with income from a land sale, the par value of such securities would gradually be divested of real worth as inflation progresses. It is generally believed that stocks can hedge the loss arising from inflation. However, farmers are usually wary of the risks involved in investing in stocks and by instinct prefer land over precious metals and jewels.

Because target profits rule the behaviors of untapped landowners, the volume of land supply can be said to tend to decrease in contrast with the rise in market price, no matter whether or not the cost involved in land sale is proportional and whether the proportion is progressive or regressive, which thus shows the supply curve sloping negative.

In order to explain the upward sloped supply curve, the law of diminishing returns (law of progressive cost) and the postulate of profit maximization were essential. However, in order to explain the minus sloped supply curve in the case of the untapped land market, the postulate of target profit by itself is sufficient.

Ethos of Economic Behavior

What should be questioned in this connection is whether the postulate of profit maximization—or the postulate of satisfaction maximization—is infallibly appropriate as the principle for human behavior. Max Weber in his *The Ethics of Protestantism and the Spirit of Capitalism* referred to farm workers in Silesia to point out that unlike British workers they tended to rest one day out of every two days if their cropshare is doubled. Japanese farmers can be said to have something in common with these Europeans in that they do not seek the maximization of satisfaction in economic terms.

In this connection, it is necessary to go back to the substance of profit in order to understand why the principle of profit maximization has been accepted as a general postulate in economics. To simplify the background, let us tentatively assume that society consists of capitalists, landowners, and laborers. Within society, those who were most keenly aware of the postulate of profit maximization as the principle of economic behavior may have been industrial capitalists. Because rapid progress was achieved in the area of industrial technology as its size expanded, the accumulation of greater profits always paved the way for adopting more productive technology than before. In this context, less capital meant a danger of losing in the competition: The maximization of profit assured capitalists that they would survive through competition in the area where the effects of technical progress and the economies of scale prevailed.

In the area of commercial service, commercial capitalists may have not been as much motivated by profit maximization as the industrial capitalists were, since technical progress was relatively slow and the economies of scale were not as dominant as in the industrial area or in the current age of revolutionized distribution by large-store chains. Of course, commercial service is at times subject to regional monopoly, and there is no wonder that the commercial capitalists who were pressed under the need for expanding business size in correspondence to the expansion of regional demand acted according to the law of profit maximization in an attempt to maintain their monopolistic control over the entry of exterior capital into the regional markets.

In an assumed case—though such a case was impossible in Japan—where agricultural capitalists rented land from landowners for agricultural production with laborers employed therein, such a capitalist may have had to fear defeat in competition with other agricultural capitalists unless he updated operations with new technology, as was the case of the industrial capitalists. It should be noted that an agricultural capitalist with more productive technology (including soil improvement) can potentially pay higher rent than his competitors, and therefore he can negotiate with landowners who have landlease contracts with others to switch the contracts over to him at higher rents. Here again, the maximization of profit is essential to survive through competition.

In the banking area, however, the need for profit maximization is relatively limited, since technical progress has been insignificant in this area, except for the recent introduction of computerized on-line systems, and economy of scale is also not generally applicable. Of course, banking capitalists try to grant as many loans as possible in the most profitable areas rather than low profit areas; therefore, they appear to be seeking profit maximization. In fact, their behaviors can be said to merely reflect the competition among industrial capitalists for profit maximization.

Roughly speaking, the motive of capitalists for profit maximization is tantamount to the motive for higher accumulation because, as Weber commented, their motive for seeking profit is not necessary for more consumption, as is obvious from the virtue of frugality in consumption. In the long-term aspect, capitalists compete with one another for capital accumulation. Therefore, they have to seek profit maximization on the short-term basis in order to win in the competition for accumulation.

Is the principle of profit maximization also applicable to other social classes? For example, landowners only receive rents for their own lands subject to the competition among agricultural capitalists for more productive land. As long as a landowner keeps his land, he is free of a fear of losing in the competition. Even if he gains extra profit, he would be able neither to begin capital-based industrial operation nor to manage it as a financial asset. Therefore, he does not have a strong need for maximizing rent. Even if he tries to do so, he cannot even increase rents, unless an agricultural capitalist as a rent payer agrees to the proposal. In this case, the landowner appears to be trying to maximize rent, but his effort can be said to merely reflect mainly the competition among agricultural capitalists.

In the area of labor, laborers usually carry out their personal lives at the expense of their wage income. Even if they want to maximize their wage incomes, they have no recourse to do so. Though it is accepted by all orthodox economists, the proposition that the length of work hours can be determined by workers to maximize the difference between satisfaction derived from wage and the pains accompanying labor can be called lame logic because there is no way to quantify the satisfaction and pain involved. The only rationale or maximization of the difference between satisfaction and pains is the utilitarian presumption itself that people must behave to make their satisfaction maximum.

The principle or the ethos of profit maximization or satisfaction maximization is applicable to capitalists or small manufacturers who intend to turn into capitalists, but it is not a common principle of behavior for all people in capitalist societies. Those who behave in conformity with this principle may be called rational *homo economicus,* but there is no justification for thinking that others are irrational. Insofar as farmers in the Japanese metropolitan areas can be ascertained to act in accordance with the postulate of target profit, it may be said to remain within the category of economics if analyzed on the basis of this postulate.

Section 4. The Position of Real Estate Companies

Volume of Land Retained by Real Estate Companies

Table 3.16. shows how much land was retained by real estate businesses as of the end of 1977. Though the total of their retained land in Japan was around 300,000 hectares, its acreage in the UPA in the National Capital Sphere was only around 7,000 hectares, which was about one-tenth of the acreage of land owned in the UPA and by farmer households, but about seven times as large as the total of land annually coming under developers' projects (not the acreage of newly developed housing land as referred to in Section 1 but the acreage "under development" work, including the public-use spaces). In other words, the 7,000 hec-

Table 3.16.
Land Held by Private Developers (1977)
(*Hectares*)

	UPA	UCA	Unidentified	Outside CPA	Total
Tokyo area	7,009	8,553	1,213	4,202	20,977
Osaka area	2,340	3,483	3,033	10,121	18,977
Nagoya area	7,873	7,193	1,744	14,554	31,364
Others	16,338	25,560	14,365	181,717	237,980
Total	33,560	44,789	20,355	210,594	309,298

Source: Japanese Ministry of Construction, *A Survey on Real Estate Dealers.*

tares that real estate companies held in the UPA in the National Capital Sphere can be called a stock of raw material from which they could continue supplying annually around 1,000 hectares of newly developed housing land over a period of seven years. Therefore, the housing land companies could be called the processors who stand between untapped landowners and housing land end users. Insofar as the quantitative distribution of untapped land and developed housing land was concerned, they could not raise land prices (even though they might have intended to do so by limiting supply) once land supply from farmers increased. On the contrary, even if they try to increase supply, for instance, by emptying stock, the housing land supply would taper off if farmers stopped supplying untapped land. In this sense, the widely heard accusation that such companies are the arch-culprit of all the housing land difficulties can be said to be unfounded.

What would occur if real estate companies and not farmers dominated large acreages of land in the National Capital Sphere and if land prices fluctuated subject to their behavior? Land prices would certainly rise once all companies temporarily stopped the land supply. Even so, however, they cannot actualize gains from price rises unless they actually supply land, and they would sooner or later have to sell, since they have to cover their personnel expenses as well as interest payments while the land supply is frozen (this makes them different from farmers, who are free of such cost). If they offer land all at once, land prices might turn even downward and thus in the worst case leave no profit behind after the freeze. Therefore, what they would sell would be logically limited to an acreage sufficient to pay their costs. In this case, if land prices are still expected generally to rise at an annual rate higher than the interest rate, users (including real estate companies) may compete for buying the limited land even at the risk of borrowing from banks, thus further pressing land prices higher. However, the land price rise expands the denominator of the fractional number, which determines the annual price rise rate of land, and slows down the rise of land price. It thus brings the annual land price rise rate closer to the interest rate sooner or later, and fund requirements for land purchases may rise along with demand expansion for land, pressing interest rates upward. On the contrary, if the annual land price increase rate falls below the interest rate, no user would borrow money to buy land, and suppliers would sell land to shift from land to profit-bearing securities, thus turning land prices downward under the pressure of oversupply. However, insofar as there are people who really need housing land, the downturn of land prices would hit the bedrock at an appropriate level, and the annual price rise rate of land should nearly be equilibrated with the prevailing interest rate.

If real estate developers hold large acreages of land and can overwhelmingly affect land prices, the annual price rise rate of land and general interest rates should eventually come into equilibrium, though they might temporarily move apart. From 1960 to the oil crisis of 1973, however, the annual price rise rate of land in the National Capital Sphere had been always far above the general interest rate level. The fact that the annual price rise rate of land continued much higher than the interest rate level is evidence that real estate companies had insufficient power to manage land prices.

It is clear that the main cause of continued land price rises in the National Capital Sphere was attributable not to such companies but to their peculiar pattern of behaviors of untapped landowners, analyzed earlier. What the companies did in this circumstance was only to gain as much profit as they could under the given conditions. In this respect real estate developers and dealers indulged in such unfair trade practices as so-called land rolling among themselves for profiteering, deceptive approaches to outwit untapped landowners, selling defective houses, and issuing dishonest advertisements to deceive consumers. Yet it is unfair to attribute all the causes of housing land price rises in the National Capital Sphere only to developers and dealers in the real estate business.

Responsibility of Real Estate Companies

Real estate companies were, nevertheless, accountable for having other impacts. First of all, in the period of the *Building a New Japan* boom, they hunted about for land across the country in an attempt to merely increase the acreage of land in their possession without assured prospects for development and marketing. There is no doubt that their speculation-based purchases sped up the land price rises. In this period, the arch-cause of abnormal land price rises in Japan was the expansion of the acreage of land in their possession. It should be noted in this respect that their land purchases at that time were mainly not within the three major metropolitan regions in Japan and that even when the purchases were in such regions, the purchased lands were often not in UPAs. It should also be noted, however, that there had been no notable expansion in the acreage of land in their possession before the boom period. Therefore, it is illogical to claim that such companies were responsible for the housing land price rises in the major urban regions througout the high economic growth period.

The second point that should be noted is the weight of interest payment in the housing land development costs. Generally speaking, the ratio of net worth to total capital of Japanese firms is low compared with their counterparts in other countries. This is especially so with respect to the real estate service businesses (in 1978 the average ratio of net worth to total capital in the real estate businesses was 9.9 percent, while the all-industry average was 15.4 percent), which means that the ratio of interest payment against their total sales was extremely high (20.2 percent in 1978). This, of course, raised the sale prices of housing land to end users. According to a cost calculation that the Urban Development Association (a trade organization of major real estate companies) conducted recently on the basis of its fact-finding survey, the development cost of Yen 16,500 for untapped land per sq m as at 1975 would add up to Yen 91,900 at the time of its sale to an end user, provided that the time of its sale is six years later and that the effective utilization of untapped land into housing land is 55 percent. The percentage cost components of this cost are 30.1 percent for untapped land, 36.4 percent for civil engineering work cost, 22.4 percent for interest payment, 3.0 percent for sales and general administration expenses, and 8.1 percent for public charges. If a 5 percent profit margin is added on this cost, the sale price would be Yen 96,500.[3] Actually, however, with the real estate companies and other enterprises holding large acreages of land they had purchased during the *Building a New Japan* boom period as well as huge borrowings for these purchases, the average gestation period of untapped land, including land disqualified for development, is longer than six years, and, therefore, the weight of the interest payment in the development cost should be much higher than the above given percentage. Roughly speaking, one-fifth of the developed land price that an end user pays is tagged for the financial institutions. In other words, a part of the amount paid by newly developed land buyers flows into the richer households that already own residential houses plus financial assets. In this aspect, high land prices can be said to have played an important role for lopsided income redistribution.

Section 5. Characteristics of End-Users of Housing Land

Survey of House Owners

In comparison with the behaviors of farmer households and real estate companies, it is useful to look also at housing land end users. Kiyoshi Yamazaki, Yoshio Fuse, and Yasue Kobayashi, of the Better Living Information Center, conducted a detailed survey in the newly developed suburban housing areas near Tokyo and focused on those who newly owned houses.[4] This section summarizes some of the results of their survey, which targeted the following areas where housing construction made notable progress since around 1971.

> *Saginuma Area in Yokohama City.* An area about twenty minutes on foot from Saginuma Station of the Denen-Toshi Line, where a major private railway company provided plots with ready-to-live houses for sale;
>
> *Tsunashima Area in Yokohama City.* An area about twenty minutes on foot from Tsunashima Station of the To-Yoko Line, where a major private railway company provided housing plots as well as plots with ready-to-live houses for sale;
>
> *Nishi-Sakado Area in Sakado Town.* An area close to Ipponmatsu Station of the Ogose Line, which is a branch from the Tojo Line, where a medium-level developer provided housing land plots with ready-to-live houses for sale;
>
> *Tsurugashima Area in Tsurugashima Town.* An area about ten minutes on foot from Sakado Station of the Tojo Line, where medium- and small-size developers provided plots with ready-to-live houses;
>
> *Oeda Area in Kasukabe City.* The area about twenty minutes on foot from Sengendai Station of the Tobu Isezaki Line, where medium- and small-size developers provided relatively small lots with ready-to-live houses.

The questionnaired households were 250 each in Saginuma, Tsunashima, Nishi-Sakado, and Tsurugashima and 500 in Oeda, and a total of 1,228 replies were recovered. The survey was conducted in September 1977.

Special Characteristics of New House-Owners

By profession, 80 percent of the householders in the survey were white-collar; the next-largest group included managers of medium- and small-size firms, and then independent store and service shop proprietors. The average household size was 3.8 persons, and the average age of householders forty years.

The average annual household income of new house-owners varies from one area to another, ranging from Yen 6,970,000 in Tsunashima, Yen 6,300,000 in Saginuma, Yen 3,950,000 in Nishi-Sakado, Yen 3,420,000 in Oeda, and Yen 3,140,000 in Tsurugashima. The householders earn around 90 percent of the total household incomes, except for Oeda where the householders earn 80 percent; the rest of their income was earned by other household members.

Around 70 percent of this group purchased ready-to-live houses with plots, 20 percent purchased the plots but built the houses on custom orders, and 10 percent bought the lots with already-lived-in houses.

As Table 3.17. shows, the acquired houses were larger in size in Saginuma and Tsunashima but notably smaller in Tsurugashima and Oeda, with Nishi-Sakado positioned in-between. In Tsurugashima and

Table 3.17.
Number of Houses by Size

Target Area	Saginuma	Tsunashima	Nishisakado	Tsurugashima	Oeda	Total
Sample	205	200	202	149	329	1,085
Acreage of plot						
– 70 m^1	—	—	2	29	90	121
70–100	1	2	7	68	168	246
100–130	1	4	10	27	52	94
130–160	9	50	78	6	9	152
160–200	136	93	82	8	5	324
200–	55	51	21	7	3	137
No answer	3	—	2	4	2	11
(Mean value)	(189.5)	(182.5)	(164.8)	(103.3)	(86.6)	(140.6)
Area of floor						
– 50 m^2	—	—	20	26	72	118
50– 70	—	15	104	78	176	373
70– 90	64	43	48	27	47	229
90–110	127	69	12	10	17	235
110–	11	73	14	6	14	118
No answer	3	—	4	2	3	12
(Mean value)	(97.4)	(106.3)	(70.0)	(64.9)	(61.5)	(78.7)
Number of rooms						
– 2	—	1	8	7	11	27
3	—	2	88	90	211	391
4	15	52	68	47	80	262
5	141	66	27	4	20	258
6–	49	77	9	1	7	143
No answer	—	2	2	—	—	4
(Mean value)	(5.2)	(5.2)	(3.8)	(3.3)	(3.4)	(4.1)

Source: The Better Living Information Center

Oeda, around two-thirds of the acquired houses were with housing plots less than 100 sq m, and total housing floor spaces were less than 70 sq m.

Of these new settlers, about 40 percent in Saginuma and Tsunashima and about 20 percent in the other areas lived in owned houses prior to their movement to the newly acquired houses. Ten percent of them in Oeda and 20 percent of them in the other areas previously lived in the housing facilities that had been provided by employers. The rest of them lived mostly in rental houses or rental apartment houses. It should be noted that around one-half of those in Tsurugashima and Oeda had been either in privately owned rental houses or rental apartment houses. In Nishi-Sakado, 40 percent of them had been in privately owned apartment houses, and 10 percent had been in the rental apartment houses of the Japan Housing Corporation or local public housing corporations. Around one-half of them had their previous residences in Tokyo, and the rest had previous residences in the same prefectures as their current residences. However, only one-quarter of the householders had their birthplaces in Tokyo or Yokohama.

Their current housing conditions are certainly better than the previous ones (see Table 3.18.), especially in terms of tatami-mat space, which shows a 50 percent increase. However, current commuting hours are obviously longer for those with new homes in areas other than their previous locations.

Such improvement of housing conditions increased expenses per household, which on average amounted to Yen 13,790,000 (see Table 3.19.). According to the area breakdown, the cost was the highest in Saginuma at over Yen 20 million per household, then from Yen 12.5 million to Yen 20 million in Tsunashima, and largely from Yen 5 million to Yen 12.5 million in Nishi-Sakado, Tsurugashima, and Oeda. Roughly speaking, the cost was equivalent to around 3.5 times of the householder's annual income. The downpayment averaged 40 percent of the purchase cost in all areas, but this percentage was somewhat higher in Saginuma and Tsunashima. What lay behind the higher downpayment in the two areas was not only that the income level of householders in these areas was higher but also that more of the householders therein had owned houses elsewhere than in the other areas prior to their acquisition of the current houses and therefore could raise a larger downpayment by selling the previously owned houses.

The largest borrowing sources were commercial financial institutions, and about one-half of the households borrowed funds from such institutions. They also procured funds by borrowing from parents, siblings, and employers; this type of source covered 20 percent of the borrowed funds, which suggests that householders procured funds by borrowing

Table 3.18.
Comparison of Present House with Previous House

Target area		Saginuma	Tsunashima	Nishisakado	Tsurugashima	Oeda	Total
Acreage of plot (sq m)	Previous House	144.8	183.5	117.0	76.4	80.0	132.4
	Present House	189.5	182.5	164.8	103.3	86.6	140.6
Area of floor (sq m)	Previous House	70.5	85.0	50.4	52.6	55.4	67.6
	Present House	97.4	106.3	70.0	64.9	61.5	78.7
Number of rooms	Previous House	3.6	3.7	2.5	2.5	2.4	2.9
	Present House	5.2	5.2	3.8	3.3	3.4	4.1
Commuting time (minutes)	Previous House	54	51	45	44	47	48
	Present House	63	61	75	69	69	67

Source: The Better Living Information Center

Table 3.19.
Number of Household by Level of Acquisition Cost

Target Area	Saginuma	Tsunashima	Nishisakado	Tsurugashima	Oeda	Total
Acquisition cost						
– 5 million yen	—	1	16	9	45	71
5 – 7.5	—	—	40	16	74	130
7.5–10	—	3	49	64	69	185
10 –12.5	—	23	46	46	65	180
12.5–15	—	45	28	7	42	122
15 –20	—	70	17	2	16	105
20 –25	80	27	—	—	—	107
25 –30	101	9	—	—	—	110
30 –	13	11	1	—	—	25
(Mean Value)	(26.7)	(17.2)	(9.8)	(9.3)	(8.9)	(13.8)
Ratio of acquisition cost to annual income of household						
–1	—	4	5	2	2	13
1–2	1	29	44	9	68	151
2–3	16	60	66	40	77	259
3–4	50	35	43	50	65	243
4–5	55	22	23	25	42	167
5–6	25	6	7	8	17	63
6–	34	12	4	5	19	74
(Mean Value)	(4.9)	(3.1)	(2.8)	(3.5)	(3.3)	(3.5)
Average annual income of household (thousand yen)	5990	6070	3650	2730	2870	4070
Average loan (thousand yen)	13210	8150	6510	6090	5370	7660

Source: The Better Living Information Center

as much as permissible. Therefore, the average amount of total repayment reaches as high as Yen 890,000, approximately 20 percent of annual household incomes, and among them are those whose repayments exceed 30 percent of their annual incomes. About one-half of the housewives of these households work for increased revenues, and about one-third of householders have started either working overtime or doing extra work at home in order to earn more income.

Motives for Acquiring Houses

Then what are the reasons for acquiring owned houses at the cost of such extraordinary efforts? The authors of the report comment as follows (Yamazaki, Fuse, and Kobayashi 1977:57):

> The reasons for individual households to acquire owned houses are diverse, ranging, for instance, from the needs for psychological stability, better housing conditions and environment, insurance or assurance for better future

living, and even the means for expressing identity. The implication herein is that the purpose of acquisition of houses is not merely to own the facilities to live in but involves to a large extent the function of housing for individual satisfaction. Such a psychological tendency seems to be particularly strong among the households of lower income brackets.

After acquiring houses at such tremendous cost, however, the house-owners still have many dissatisfactions. For instance, 70 percent of them are dissatisfied with the limited space of their housing lots. Dissatisfactions with the limited space of their houses and the structures thereof, with housing equipment, and with the environment and the availability of urban life are held, respectively, among 67, 62, and 87 percent of them. More than 80 percent of the households in Tsurugashima and Oeda are dissatisfied in all these matters.

Therefore, being asked about the intention of living in the currently owned houses for lifetime, only 27 percent of them definitely answered yes, while 35 percent of them said that they would move out sooner or later. The rest of them had not decided this question. It should be noted above all that 40 to 50 percent of them in Nishi-Sakado, Tsurugashima, and Oeda intended to move out of the currently owned houses.

Notwithstanding, 69 percent of the households are satisfied with their acquisition of houses, which exceeds the percentage of those that are dissatisfied. Despite the substantial difficulties that must be overcome in order to purchase a house, the households in relatively younger age groups and lower income brackets have bought their houses, perhaps because they found the houses a status symbol and thought that such houses would become their footing to acquire better houses in the future. In this respect, the authors of the report made the following comments (1977:96–98):

In the aspect of the motives for acquisition of houses, the households in lower income brackets had a stronger desire for the actualization of expected economic merits and the stabilization of living, thus leading them to attach more importance to the acquisition of the house itself than to its comfortability. The social conditions of housing at present conceivably urge these household groups to the acquisition of owned houses sooner and by all means. Therefore, in answer to a question about what they think about the next houses and what they intend to do of the currently owned houses, more than 90% of households which intend to move out of the current houses "within 5 years" expressed their preference for independent houses and the intention of selling their current houses to buy new houses. Therefore, a sizable segment of the households in lower income brackets acquired their currently owned houses at the cost of extraordinary efforts in the hope that these houses would offer a footing for acquiring better houses at the next stage, thus representing their desire for attaining economic merits and more stable living.

This explains, in turn, that though they find dissatisfactions with many specific points of their currently owned houses which are qualitatively inferior, they are more satisfied with the acquisition of owned houses itself.

The Role of Increased Land Prices in Income Redistribution

The most notable of all the problems arising from increased land prices is the expansion of income disparity between the households that have land to sell and those that have no such land. Because of high land prices, a large majority of households cannot acquire houses to live in or have to suffer under the heavy burden of repaying debts after acquiring such houses, while on the other hand a handful of households can earn huge amounts of capital gains by selling only small fragments of land in their possession. Table 3.20. shows both the personal income and the annual increase of the estimated value of land in household possession (extracted from the National Economic Accounting Report) for comparison with personal income from land sales. At 10 to 1 the ratio of the household receipt to the private income from land sale can be said to be abnormal (the ratio of the compensation of employees to the said private income is 5 to 1). Moreover, the increase in the estimated amount of land assets in household possession is larger than realized profits from land sales.

Table 3.21. shows the relationship between the household income and house acquisition cost. The acquisition cost is based on a model case for a house of 100 sq m in floor space on a 200 sq m land plot. The nominal income and the amount of saving are the averages of those for nonfarm households. The ratio of the house acquisition cost to the nominal income has annually increased, thus showing the 1976

Table 3.20
Comparison of Revenue of Household and Land Sale
(*Billions of Yens*)

Year	Revenue of household	Wages	Land sale	Annual increase of estimated value of land in household possession
1970	58,018.4	(31,001.3)	5,800	19,546.9
1971	65,794.2	(36,769.4)	8,700	19,565.7
1972	76,489.4	(42,555.8)	8,800	46,483.3
1973	95,739.9	(53,715.9)	15,200	44,703.0
1974	121,405.0	(68,030.2)	unknown	△ 1,632.5
1975	140,320.0	(79,450.8)	10,300	18,043.3
1976	158,908.6	(90,284.9)	9,800	12,769.7
1977	175,461.5	(100,782.8)	9,900	17,394.2

Source: Annual Report on National Accounts (1979) and Internal Data of Ministry of Finance.

Table 3.21
Comparison of Housing Acquisition Cost and Annual Income
(*Thousands of Yens*)

Acquisition cost		1968	1970	1973	1976
Land		4,000	8,000	12,000	18,000
(unit price)		(20)	(40)	(60)	(90)
Building		1,000	3,000	6,000	8,000
(unit price)		(10)	(30)	(60)	(80)
Total	1	5,000	11,000	18,000	26,000
Income					
Nominal Revenue	2	1,080	1,390	2,120	3,160
Nominal Saving	3	1,120	1,600	2,430	2,990
Annual Payment on Loan	4	470	1,130	1,870	2,760
2–4	5	610	260	250	400
1/2		4.6	7.9	8.4	8.2
Deflated	2	1,160	1,390	1,960	2,350
Deflated	5	660	260	200	220

ratio two times as large as the 1968 ratio. This means that the difficulty of acquiring a house has accordingly increased during this period.

What is more, most of the households must use all of their savings but still need to borrow large amounts in order to acquire houses. Supposing the repayment rate on the borrowings to be repaid at 12 percent (equivalent to 9 percent per annum of interest rate over a period of fifteen years), the amount of repayment, including the interest payment, in 1970 and thereafter would reach somewhere near 80 percent of the nominal income. With such a heavy repayment burden, no household will be sure of its economic viability. Therefore, people have to either give up their plans for house acquisition or to substantially scale down the sizes of house for acquisition. Table 3.22. shows how households scaled down their plans from year to year.

Table 3.22
Average Square Meters in Residential Plots by Year and Urban Ring

Year of land acquisition	10 km	10–20	20–30	30–40	40–50	Total
Before 1968	129	192	253	316	393	252
1970	99	137	140	177	218	157
1972	93	116	126	159	204	141
1974	103	125	148	168	202	157
1976	89	111	136	163	180	142
1978	82	103	131	149	168	131

Source: Calculated by author based on *Housing Survey* (1978) by The Prime Minister's Office.

To sum up, though the concentration of population into major cities and its outflow into suburbs continued through the high economic growth period, farmers as original housing land suppliers did not increase land supply as land prices rose, though they sold land to satisfy their incidental needs for cash income. They tended rather to decrease quantitative land supply in inverse proportion to the land price rises. As the result, in contrast with the surprising expansion of the worth of land as an asset possessed by farmer households, the actual living standard of households that acquired houses after having borrowed funds from all available sources or economized on their living expenses to save money for house acquisition, worsened notwithstanding the rise of their annual incomes along with the growth of the Japanese economy.

Notes

1. Tokyo Metropolitan Government, "Tokyo-To No Jinko Ido No Jittai" (The Present Situation of Population Movement in Tokyo Metropolis) (Tokyo Metropolitan Government: internal report, 1979).
2. Where p is market price, q is quantitative supply, and π is profit that a certain landowner aims to attain, the supply function for him can be expressed as
   $$p * q = \pi$$
   With price shown on the vertical scale and quantitative supply on the horizontal scale, equation (3.1) makes a convexwise orthogonal hyperbolic curve against the origin. In orthodox economics, the supply curve shows an upward slope, with quantitative supply increasing along with the rise of price under the law of diminishing return, provided that the generally accepted postulate of profit maximization prevails. However, in the case where the said postulate of target profit prevails, quantitative supply decreases with the rise of price.

   The acreage of available land is limited within an area where land prices are virtually on the same level, with the number of landowners also limited. Though the amounts of profit that individual landowners want to attain may not necessarily be the same with one another, if the individually required profits are predeterminable, the supply curve of land therein would be based on
   $$p(q_1 + q_2 + \dots + q_\eta) = (\pi_1 + \pi_2 + \dots + \pi_\eta)$$
   With the sum total of q replaced with Q and the sum total of π as Π, the supply function of land in this area is the same as equation (3.1), thus making the same convexwise orthogonal hyperbolic curve.
3. Toshi Kaihatsu Kyokai (Urban Development Association), *Minkan Takuchi Kaihatsu to Shakai Shihon Toshi (Private Housing Land Development and Social Capital Investment)* (Tokyo: Urban Development Association, 1977).
4. Kokumin Seikatsu Center (Better Living Information Center), "Daitoshi Shuhenbu ni Okeru Jutaku Shutoku" (Acquisition of House in the Peripheries of Major Cities) (Tokyo Metropolitan Government: internal report, 1978).

4

Policies for Better Land Use

Section 1. Preventing Sprawl

The ultimate objective of land policy is better land use. Certainly, land prices are a crucial issue, and policy for land price control is a major means to reach this target. This chapter, however, examines the various policy instruments that seem to immediately contribute to better land use. Policy instruments for land price control are discussed in Chapter 5.

Disadvantages of Sprawl

Sprawl has many disadvantages. First of all, because of sprawl, workers undergo rush-hour commuting between their suburban houses and midtown offices in extremely overcrowded transit. Many travel more than three hours daily in the National Capital Sphere; they serve their official workhours plus commuting hours. To make the situation worse, the farther their houses are from midtown offices, the less frequently do their trains run, which increases their loss of time and mental strain.

Second, sprawl contributes to worsening the local living environment. In sprawl areas, roads generally have been developed along preexisting serpentine farm lanes, which lead into loops or closed lanes that pass through new housing plots. These narrow lanes act as passageways for cars owned by new inhabitants and for trucks plying between highways and the ongoing land development sites or house building plots. They thus pose the danger of traffic accidents to workers hurrying to railway stations, housewives on their way to shopping, and even farmers who have to move between their homes and their fragmented farm plots that still remain among newly built houses. Pedestrians must guard against the splashes of passing vehicles when it rains and the dust when it is dry. Shops and houses standing near these roads are coated with muddy splashes, and farm crops become dust-coated and injured by car exhaust.

Third, sprawl significantly impairs the efficiency of public investment. The inhabitants in such an area may initially use water wells, but they soon need city water service not only because wells are inconvenient but because well water becomes contaminated by underground discharge seepage from septic tanks of nearby houses; this can cause dysentery and virus-caused hepatitis. Because farmland plots are still scattered among houses, the cost of city water service becomes much higher than it is in densely populated towns because the per house piping is much longer from the main pipeline. At the same time, along with sprawl, the inflow of polluted water into irrigational ponds and channels increases, which causes their contaminated water to emit offensive smells. This leads to the need for the construction of an extensive sewage system, which is more costly than the installation of city water piping. The pipe size of a combined sewer becomes larger along with the target area, since it also must take in rainwater. In the case of a separate sewer, the gradient of its main pipe route must be steeper than the combined sewer. The trunk pipeline close to the terminal treatment facility must be deeper than the combined sewer, which means that a larger capacity pumping system is needed. In any case, the construction cost per capita in a sprawl area becomes much higher than in a heavily populated area.

Demand for city gas also rises among inhabitants as the number of residential houses in a sprawl area increases, since propane gas is inconvenient and is subject to more danger of explosion than city gas is. However, as in the cases of city water and sewage services, the cost of installation of city gas service piping would again be higher in a sprawl area. What is more, the network of such public utilities must meet newly rising individual requirements one after another, thus leading to the need for tearing up roads frequently for piping installations and repairs, which often causes damage to the other pipings. This causes the installation, maintenance, and repair costs to rise and makes detours necessary on crowded narrow roads. There can be extra costs for the installation of electricity and telephone service lines, even though such costs might not be as high as in the cases for the installation of underground city water, sewage, and gas service pipings. It should also be noted that insufficient street lights in suburban housing areas may give rise to more crimes than the urban average.

The public service sector is not the only victim of sprawl inefficiency. The bus transportation service business cannot operate profitably in sprawl areas, which increases the number of cars that are needed and that contribute to frequent traffic jams on highways; this again interferes with bus traffic. Such services as taxi companies, shops, restaurants and coffee shops, and clinics are found less frequently in sparsely populated sprawl areas. The inhabitants in such areas therefore have less access to such services and must stand in long lines in the available shops and food service stores, for taxi service after the termination of bus service at relatively early evening hours, and the arrogance of physicians and dentists whose numbers are locally limited.

It is difficult, if not impossible, to implement a city plan in an area that has reached such a hopeless condition. Take, for instance, the expansion of a highway; the local authorities must negotiate with innumerable small-plot owners in order to acquire their small plots. Neither farmers who look forward to further land price rises nor new settlers who have obtained their housing plots after much painstaking effort would be willing to offer even tiny parts of their plots at cost for the expansion of the highway. Even if the landowners involved are persuaded, the local governments would have to provide a large fund to pay not only for the purchase of their lands but also for the expensive compensation of those who move out of the purchased plots to other places for new settlement. The Land Readjustment Scheme also cannot proceed smoothly, since a large number of small-plot owners are usually reluctant to take the risk of readjustment loss. Local governments have no choice but to remain idle in the sprawl areas, since they are financially incapable of redeveloping such areas. Even so, the remaining farm plots will gradually be fragmented for conversion into housing plots. What eventually may develop is a town that has houses side by side and that is interwoven with labyrinthine lanes that are at times inaccessible to fire engines and garbage trucks. The town may have no park or green areas but may have industrial installations that often cause disputes with the inhabitants in their neighborhood. Indeed, the existence of such towns is already common.

Sprawl areas also create aesthetic problems. Few find it attractive to look at ten to fifteen or even twenty shabby houses standing side by side in a tiny newly developed housing plot of around 1,000 sq m converted from a part of paddyfield. Very few people think it attractive to see a row of mortared wooden-frame apartment houses without trees and surrounded with washed clothes hanging out to dry, although some people praise the beauty of a rice-planted paddy surrounded completely with apartment houses or a pear garden adjoining a house-congested area. It is true that rice plants turn green in mid-summer, and pear trees bear pretty blossoms in the spring. However, such natural beauty on a limited space of land alone cannot create a beautiful town. What is more, such a small space of cultivated land is often used to justify the construction of congested houses or apartment houses because the two types of space are combined as a single area under the Building Code. After the authorization for housing construction under the code is attained, developers soon turn the small farmland space into housing land plots for the construction of more hosues. It is unreasonable to prefer a sprawl area to a well-arranged urbanization zone only because the sprawl's fragmentary farmlands among housing developed areas are beautiful. The farmlands in a sprawl area are not spaces exempted from sprawl but the remains of land that caused the house-congested suburban towns.

After all, the scattered farmlands in the UPA cannot only be called potential housing land but also land that should positively be converted into housing land by means of urbanization planning. Of course, they can in some cases be kept as public open spaces or be converted into children's playgrounds, public parks, and schoolyards. What is important is that farmlands and woodlands that can be developed into housing land whenever their owners choose are themselves the general source of random development of sprawl.

The Ecology of Sprawl

Sprawl is hard to cope with. The ongoing sprawl in the major urban regions in Japan can be classified into two types: (1) limited-size sprawling, such as sprawling into farmland and woodland within a range of around 2 kilometers from a railway station, and (2) extensive sprawling, which links limited-size sprawls one after another along both sides of a railway. The former can be called *micro-type sprawl* and the latter *macro-type sprawl*.

These two types of sprawl are mutually interactive with land prices, which play the role of parameter. With the rise of a micro-type sprawl around a railway station, the price of farmlands scattered among housing land areas also rises. Land prices within walking distance to the station rise close to buyers' marginal ability to pay (a new bus route outward from the station can seldom be opened in the sprawl area because of its limited population, unless a large housing complex is built out of the sprawl area). However, the expected users of housing land start seeking housing plots near the next railway station farther away from the urban center. As long as the annual population inflow into the major urban regions continues, the conversion of untapped land into housing land around the next station develops, thus pressing land prices higher around the next station. However, in this process, the prices of land around the other station are relatively higher than the prices of land around the next station, since the former can offer more convenience to commuters than the latter, thus reaching a level beyond the reach of expected users. As the result, the remaining farmland around the earlier referred station may be left intact. Because a sprawl's capacity for accepting new inhabitants around a station is limited, the macro-type sprawling rapidly spreads along a railway farther away from the urban center. Of course the micro-type sprawl and the macro-type sprawl actually progress in tandem. In reality, the sprawling around the second station starts while that around the first station is still under way. However, the sprawl around a railway station and around the other station interacts with the land prices around the two stations.

Zoning Game

Under the National Land Use Planning Act, the land use plans seem to have covered nearly the entire expanse of national land. The UPA and UCA have explicitly been identified, and land development is under strict control in the UCA and the Agriculture Promotion Areas. Why, then, has the just described mess occurred in the major urban regions? We have to find the answer. At the core of these problems is that urbanization causes land price rises and that control of land development deprives landowners of the opportunity to gain from increased land prices or of the expectation for gains therefrom. Therefore, city planning tends to accommodate a fait accompli, and a city plan based on such a planning is doomed to fail in achieving its objective—that is, to eliminate sprawl. Actually, when the zoning of the UPA and UCA was ready for implementation under the City Planning Law of 1969, virtually all landowners in the affected areas requested that their lands be included in the UPA, which led the UPA to be expanded over a huge total acreage of good farmland. This process can be reviewed with reference, for instance, to the case of Hachioji City in Tokyo.

The City Planning Law was promulgated on 15 June 1968, but its actual enforcement date was on 14 June 1969, one year later. (The technical standard of the zoning of the UPA and the UCA was detailed in Chapter 1.) The Tokyo metropolitan government (TMG) announced its "Policy for the Zoning of the Urbanization Promotion Area and the Urbanization Control Area" in April 1970 to make clear its basic policy for the zoning and its approach to the compilation of a draft zoning plan. TMG planned to determine the qualified areas—which were expected to have a population density of forty persons or more per hectare as of 1980—for the UPA on the basis of the following method.

The entire outskirts of Tokyo were zoned into 500 meter squares, and each grid point was appraised in terms of topographical conditions, transportation conditions, land use regulation, urbanization ratio, and the possibility of urbanization. Then with the expected population increase from 1965 to 1980 distributed to each grid point pro rata to its appraised weight, the actual population as of 1965 was added to each distributed population. In case the per hectare population at a grid

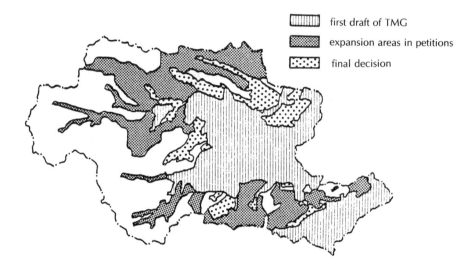

first draft of TMG

expansion areas in petitions

final decision

Figure 4.1. *Expansion of UPA in Hachioji City.*

point exceeded 300 persons, the surplus was again distributed to the adjoining grid points pro rata to their weights.

Based on these grid points, which each would have a per hectare population of forty or more persons as of 1980, TMG made public in April 1970 the First Basic Draft Plan. The total of the UPA under the First Draft was 103,000 hectares (59.5 percent of the Tokyo acreage), comprising 57,000 hectares in the twenty-three ward area (the whole of the central part of Tokyo) and 45,900 hectares in the outskirt area (39.6 percent of the area). Figure 4.1. shows the UPA and UCA in Hachioji City under the First Basic Draft Plan. The UPA acreage in the city at that time was 5,748 hectares. Hachioji City gave a local briefing on this Basic Draft in May 1970 where requests were made by many inhabitants for expanding the UPA. Following this briefing, twenty-six petitions were submitted for the inclusion of specific areas into the UPA and two for the UCA. As Figure 4.1. shows in grey, these petitions called for including virtually the whole of the city area, except for the mountainous area, into the UPA. The petitions for the UPA covered areas (excluding the duplicates) totaling 7,396 hectares, thus reaching 56.7 percent of the total acreage of the UCA under the First Basic Draft Plan.

Based on such strong requests by local inhabitants, the Mayor of Hachioji submitted petitions for UPA expansion to TMG more than once, including those signed by the mayors of three cities, the heads of six towns, and the chief of a village in the neighborhood of Hachioji, and submitted (21 May 1970) petitions to the governor of Tokyo and the president of the Tokyo Metropolitan Assembly.

Then, after referring a plan that took into consideration such petitions to the City Planning Council, the TMG announced its Second Basic Draft Plan on 15 August 1970, which incorporated most of the gentle slopes among the hills into the UPA, thus increasing the UPA acreage in Hachioji by 1,268 hectares to 7,016 hectares, or 22 percent. Still, the petitions for the expansion of the UPA continued, which led to another addition of 257 hectares to the UPA acreage in the city. In other words, the UPA acreage in Hachioji substantially expanded in response to the strong requests of local landowners.

Institutional Preconditions for Zoning

In order to effectively advance a city plan, it is necessary to accede to landowners' established interests and to go along with their expectations for future gains. Even though it may be difficult to do so, it is still necessary to minimize the differences in economic interests between the development controlled areas and the development promotion areas. In principle, two approaches can achieve this.

The first approach is to compensate the development controlled areas for the loss, but this approach is impractical. First, it is extremely difficult to estimate both current and future economic losses arising from a conceivable fall in land prices due to the control of development. Second, if compensation were legally required, its sum would certainly rise beyond the ability to pay on the part of the national treasury or the local governments. What can actually be done in this situation would be to designate the development controlled areas as, for example, the Agriculture Promotion Areas, so that the areas can be made eligible to the state budget appropriation for infrastructural arrangements in the name of promoting agriculture.

The second and more practical approach is to confiscate a part of the landowners' gains from the development. Of course, it would be ideal if the land price could be frozen with the authorization of the development. Granted that such a freeze is difficult, even some effective limitation on the gains of individual landowners would suffice.

There are restrictions on the utilization of land even in the UPA, but these restrictions are moderate compared to the control on farmland in the UCA and the Agriculture Promotion Areas. In order to ultimately balance the interests of the landowners in the UPA and the landowners in the UCA and the Agricultural Promotion Areas, it is necessary in the UPA to impose much stronger control on rights to earn gains from and to dispose of land—apart from the right to use it—than in the latter areas.

Taxation and eminent domain are the means of public control, respectively, on the right to earn from land and on the right to dispose of land. In this sense, it can logically be said that some sort of extraordinary taxation and the means of expropriation should be arranged with respect to land in the UPA. To be more specific, a higher rate of the city planning tax than the current rate should be imposed on land in the UPA. (In the case of land readjustment, projects should not be permitted unless landowners contributed with no compensation 20 to 30 percent of their land so that the contributed plots can be used for public facilities such as streets and parks: see the further discussion of land readjustment in the next section.) With such arrangements imposed, landowners would think realistically about the possible benefits of the UPA and the UCA.

Insofar as the city planning tax remains at the current low rate of 0.3 percent in the UPA—excepting farmland—with no coercion to join a land readjustment project, no landowner would be happy to have his land incorporated into the UCA, which exerts stronger control over land use than the UPA does. On the other hand, as long as virtually all landowners press for the inclusion of their lands into the UPA, it is difficult to implement a successful city plan. A definitive zoning of the UPA and the UCA—with a higher and nondiscriminatory city planning tax rate on land in the UPA and the compulsory land readjustment as preconditions—should be a fundamental principle of land policy in the areas where urbanization is in progress.

It should be noted that the land readjustment formula in the UPA can better achieve the required infrastructural urban arrangement at far cheaper cost than the land purchase formula, as will be discussed later. It should also be noted that since a higher city planning tax rate functions as significant annual cost to landowners, they cannot leave vacant land plots in the UPA intact. In this sense, it can accelerate the supply of untapped land and can, consequently, act to slow down the land price rises. These two functioning together to expedite the conversion of untapped land plots in the UPA into housing areas can help weaken the moves of landowners for converting the UCA into the UPA and thus help preserve nature therein.

Section 2. Attaining Public Space for a Good Living Environment

The Concept of Land Readjustment

A good living environment requires public spaces. Parks help provide relaxation, and streets provide garbage trucks, fire engines, and ambulances access to individual residences; they are indispensable for the maintenance of comfortable urban living. However, acquisition of such public spaces in the housing land development areas is becoming costly for local governments because of increased land prices and the egocentric resistance of landowners.

As was mentioned earlier, eminent domain is the most effective policy for immediately achieving the required acquisition of public spaces. But land acquisition by execution of eminent domain requires just compensation and, therefore, large appropriations from local governmental funds. In this respect, the land readjustment formula in Japan is a reliable policy instrument for arranging urban area. Incorporated in this formula is communal contribution through replotting procedures, which is a variety of expropriation. This section analyzes the problems involved in this formula on the premise that it is an instrument to acquire necessary public space for the maintenance of a good urban living environment.

When landowners are the main promoters of a land readjustment project, the purpose of the project is to bring forth expected economic effects. That is, by contributing their land without compensation for public works like roads and parks, they intend to increase the value of the rest of their plots. Where there is only one landowner involved, for instance, he or she can best achieve this purpose by deciding on the locations and shapes of such public units so that the value of the remaining private units minus the development and other costs can be maximized. However, where there are two landowners or more, what is additionally required is to redistribute the newly developed plots (replotting) on an equitable basis so that they can fairly share the increased values arising from the readjustment.

Insofar as the price of land—which represents its value—is understood as the amount of consideration that users pay for its usefulness, the best development of a housing area for end users can be said to also be in the best interests of landowners. This is the basic philosophy underlying the concept of land readjustment. Communal contribution and land replotting are characteristics of the land readjustment formula that clearly differentiate it from the land purchase formula as a policy instrument for urban development.[1]

For simplification's sake, suppose a case where landowners A, B, and C own the same acreage of land (Aa = Ab = Ac) each, as shown in the top portion of Figure 4.2. (the broken lines are boundaries of the parcels) and the hatched space for the construction of a street decreases their land spaces, respectively, to A'a, A'b, and A'c. Assume that the unit land price within the figure before the street construction equals P and that the unit land price therein after the street construction is P'. The prices of land plots owned by A, B, and C before the construction are respectively, P*Aa, P*Ab, and P*Ac, and the relevant postconstruction prices are P'*A'a, P'*A'b, and P'*A'c.

In case the land purchase formula is adopted on the basis of a unit price of P paid for the street space, A, B, and C respectively receive the amounts P(Aa − A'a), P(Ab − A'b), and P(Ac − A'c). Then the increase in the amount of property value for A after the street construction is P'A'a + P(Aa − A'a) − PAa = (P' − P)A'a. The postconstruction unit price of land is, of course, larger than the pre-construction unit price, thus P' − P > 0. Therefore, the increase in the amount of property value for A is equal to the remaining acreage in A's possession multiplied by the unit price increase. The same can be said with B and C.

However, as is evident from Figure 4.2.(1), the B-owned acreage after the construction (A'b) is far smaller than the A- or C-owned post-construction acreage (A'a) or (A'c). In other words, although the pre-

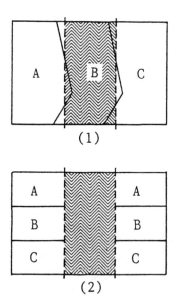

Figure 4.2. *Concept of land readjustment.*

construction property amounts were the same, B alone has less increase in the amount of postconstruction property, thus evidencing the presence of inequity under this land purchase formula. In order to eliminate this inequity, the unit purchase price should be set at P' instead of P. In other words, in order to attain agreement from the landowners involved, it is necessary to pay P', the unit price expected for realization after the street construction. Even if P' is paid as the unit purchase price, what may be left for B after the construction are three smaller plots in irregular shapes, as compared with the single larger and relatively normal-shaped land plots for A and C, thus still leaving disadvantages on the part of B. On the other hand, in case the area is replotted for redistribution among A, B, and C under the land readjustment formula, as the bottom portion of Figure 4.2. shows, required equity among them can virtually be achieved. To sum up, the land readjustment formula is superior to the land purchase formula in that it can minimize inevitable inequities among the interested parties.

In this case, insofar as their postconstruction gains from increased land prices are larger than the losses arising from their free land contribution to communal street spaces (setting aside the construction cost as negligible in this case), the public street construction is advantageous to landowners A, B, and C. In other words, the construction of a communal street at the cost of land contribution brings forth benefits to landowners through increased unit land prices.[2]

In the case of the land purchase formula the actual purchase price P' is closer to the postconstruction unit price, since it would hardly be possible to attain agreement from all the interested landowners if the purchase price were set at the preconstruction unit price P. However, in the case of the land readjustment formula, the objective can be achieved without paying the costs of purchasing land.

If no compensation is paid for the public street spaces, the landowners may complain that the formula is extremely disadvantageous to them. However, since in the case of the land purchase formula persons other than the landowners must bear the purchase cost, their complaints imply that they are entitled to gain a windfall at the cost of a third party. Moreover, since landowners can expect to gain from increased land prices in the case of land readjustment because of the public street constructions at least equal to the value of the lost acreage of land, this formula is not particularly disadvantageous to them provided that their forthcoming profits are sufficiently large. Communal contribution through land readjustment is a variety of land expropriation that distributes the cost of arranging public facilities among the interested persons as equitably as feasible under the given circumstances. It initially obligates landowners to bear a part or the whole of the cost for providing a public street or other public facilities on the grounds that they can expect gains from increased postconstruction unit land prices. Ultimately, the cost will of course be paid by the end users of the land plots involved either as land price or rent.

As is discernible from the prescribed characteristics of land readjustment, the participants in such projects were originally the owners of large land acreages who could expect more gains than they might lose through communal contribution. However, the general and radical land price rises in the major urban regions, a consequence of the rapid population concentration in such regions throughout the high economic growth period, remarkably changed the psychology of landowners. They grew reluctant to participate in land readjustment projects. Even without joining in the complicated procedures involved in such a project, they could certainly expect annual land price increases of over 20 percent and their own land plots seemed certain to become more valuable in the future.[3]

When the land readjustment formula lost its attraction for landowners, the municipalities had to become the promoters of the land readjustment projects because they could not ignore the wayward progress of urbanization in their jurisdictions. However, they encountered strong resistance from landowners against the readjustment projects, under circumstances of general and radical land price rises. Unless effective measures are provided to reduce such resistance, it is difficult to promote land readjustment. Since it is unlikely that the elected mayors of municipalities will resolutely stand against landowners who act on the basis of economic need, the implementation of land readjustment projects is actually limited to very small areas, and random urbanization to a large extent is left free.

The most controversial problem in land readjustment is always the reduction in plot area. This system is currently based in principle on the prorated distribution of the required costs among the landowners and the figuratively estimated increments in value of land plots per landowner. However, insofar as this principle is followed on the basis of the estimated incremental benefits only in terms of land price, even the owner of a small housing plot, for instance, will be obligated to contribute his tiny share, even though this space is indispensable to his household. In such a case, the landowner can be permitted to pay his share in cash, but at times, he might be short of this cash. What is more, in the case of an interarea highway, the main beneficiaries are often not the residents in the land readjustment zone. In such a case, the landowners affected are supposed to bear the burden attributable to the highway space, thus causing inequity between the landowners and the main beneficiaries.

The Principle of Burden Prorated to Ability to Pay

This private plot reduction system may benefit from allowing the burden to be prorated according to individual ability to pay. If it is substituted for the current space reduction formula, which is prorated to expected individual benefits, small housing plot owners would be excused from the burden of reduction. By regarding such a formula of contribution as a kind of tax, the concept of the tax exemption limit or the basic allowance can be applied to such small plot owners. It may also be feasible to standardize the communal contribution rate at around 20 percent by limiting the reserve acreage to the required spaces for the in-zone streets and parks while excluding the trunk highway space from the readjustment requirements.

As for the creation of trunk highways and the sewage treatment area among many readjustment zones, these can be arranged through integration of the reserved spaces, which the readjustment project promoters may prepare by advance purchase or by securing extra spaces beyond the 20 percent contribution rate. The project promoters' payments should be made as cash reimbursements to individual landowners for their extra contribution.

Under the current system, in addition to the contribution for public uses, individual landowners are obligated jointly to reserve extra land for sale intended to build a fund for civil engineering and construction costs. If this financial resource system is abolished, municipalities would bear the cost; they can raise the city planning tax rates to cover this cost. (I shall later introduce a trial estimate to illustrate this point.)

Since a 20 percent reduction rate is considerably lower than the currently prevailing rate, which is over 30 percent in most of the land readjustment projects, and since small housing plot owners would be exempt from the obligation of plot reduction, the resistance on the part of landowners to such projects will presumably be weakened, thus facilitating the promotion land readjustment projects that are now politically impossible. What is more, with the burden prorated to ability to pay, the landowners can expect to have postreadjustment plots in principle close to their prereadjustment plots in exchange for 20 percent reduction on each plot, thus leading to much easier compilation of the replotting plan and less discontent among landowners about the replotting than under the current system, which is based on the principle of burden prorated to expected benefit.

However, such a substantial revision of the contribution system is impossible unless the land readjustment system is made legally compulsory throughout UPA. Enforcing the principle of burden prorated to ability to pay only in the areas where the land readjustment projects are accepted while leaving the other areas intact would obviously run counter to the principle of equity. In this connection, it will become necessary to apply the contribution system mutatis mutandis to the housing development projects by private developers so that they are also obligated to contribute the public use spaces without compensation. Then, it will be necessary to prohibit housing construction in the areas where no land readjustment has been implemented.

Currently, with the acreage annually coming under the land readjustment projects still limited, it is practically impossible to prohibit housing construction in the areas where the land readjustment system has not been applied yet. Because housing construction is currently permitted even in such areas, landowners prefer to avoid the trouble of land readjustment, which spreads reluctance to accept land readjustment. This boomerangs by scaling down the acreage coming under land readjustment projects. The indispensable conditions for disrupting this vicious cycle are to radically expand the size of areas in which land readjustment applies and to raise the city planning tax rates in order to secure the funds to finance thus expanded land readjustment projects. In this case the city planning tax must be raised to a sufficiently high level to follow the rise of land prices in the land readjustment completed areas in order to prevent landowners therein from leaving newly developed plots intact or using these as farmland only in an attempt to earn larger gains from land price rises.

Section 3. Improving Municipal Finances in Areas of Increasing Population

Population Expansion and Local Government

As Dr. Shoup earnestly emphasized in his recommendation to the supreme commander of occupation forces in Japan after World War II, local autonomy is the foundation of grass-roots democracy. Therefore, as was mentioned in Chapter 2, he recommended that the base of local government finance be strengthened. Along with population concentration in major cities and population flow into the suburbs after World War II, farm villages in the vicinities of major cities rapidly turned into so-called dormitory cities. Even without Shoup's recommendation, it was obvious that the establishment of a firm financial basis of local governments in these areas was essential for a deep-rooted democracy in Japan. Without such a financial basis, the local governments would have to rely on financial aid from the central government and the prefectural governments to meet the increasing requirements of inhabitants. Both the local governments and legislatures would have to be receptive to the political pressure from both the state and the prefectures, thus diverging from the principle of local autonomy. In fact, however, the financial position of municipalities in the population-expanding areas at that time was extremely tight. A good illustration is the case of the city of Machida in Tokyo.

Machida before 1965 was an assemblage of typical farm villages in the vicinity of Tokyo. Hara-Machida as its central town had been a local commercial center, with exchange markets opening periodically, since the Edo Era and had maintained brisk commercial service for the soldiers and employees of the United States forces garrisoned at Sagamihara Camp near the city after World War II. However, the city population as of 1960 was around 70,000 persons—around 100,000 with the population in its peripheries included.

With the enforcement of the National Capital Sphere Arrangement Law in 1957, Machida was designated as one of the satellite cities of Tokyo to positively receive more population from the densely inhabited midtown area. Beginning with the construction of the Kogasaka Housing Complex by the Tokyo Housing Supply Corporation in 1961 (occupation by tenants completed in 1965) as the first large housing complex in Machida, large housing development projects were launched one after another—seven complexes by the Tokyo Housing Supply Corporation, four complexes by the Japan Housing Corporation, seven complexes by the Tokyo metropolitan government, and two complexes by the Machida municipal government itself. Together with the progress of housing land development by private developers and the land readjustment projects with landowners participating, the city population has increased explosively to the current level of around 280,000 persons. That is, the city population quadrupled in the twenty years since 1960.

The expansion of the city population caused pressing demand for various urban facilities. First of all, the Odakyu Line, which was the only commuter train line connecting Machida City and the business center in Tokyo, experienced chaotic traffic congestion during rush hours, with each coach carrying triple its specified maximum passengers. About two-thirds of commuters from the housing complex areas to the railway stations used buses as the means of transportation, but construction of bus terminals in front of these stations and roads lagged behind the expansion of bus traffic. The road space ratio to the acreage of the UPAs as of 1978 was only 9 percent, and the road density was 210 meters per hectare. Moreover, only one-quarter of the roads were 5.5 meters or more in width.

The shortage of public parks and sewage facilities was not unique to Machida City but was a general phenomenon in the midtown area as well as the suburbs of Tokyo. Still, the situation in Machida City was one of the worst. The park space ratio was only 0.8 percent of the UPA in acreage, and the per capita park space was as small as 1.6 sq m. The sewage service acreage was 3 percent, covering 10 percent of the city population, as of 1978.

It is true that the Machida municipal government (MMG) made tremendous efforts to tackle the shortage of urban facilities. For instance, the number of compulsory education facilities as of 1960—twelve primary schools (207 classes) and six junior high schools (101 classes)—was nearly tripled as of 1978—thirty-six primary schools (908 classes) and twelve junior high schools (207 classes). The percentage share of the educational budget appropriations in the annual expenditures of the MMG exceeded 30 percent (38.6 percent in 1971), thus substantially surpassing 20 percent of its civil engineering and construction expenditures and approximately equaling 10 percent of the total budget for welfare, public hygiene, general administration, and redemption of city bonds.

The size of the MMG's budget increased by twenty-one times from Yen 1,700 million in FY 1965 to Yen 35,500 million in FY 1978. With the population increased by 2.5 times and general prices increased by around two times in the same period taken into account, the size of the city's budget in that period can be said to have been approximately quadrupled per capita in real terms (Figure 4.3.).

Of these resources, local tax revenues and the inhabitant tax revenue also increased by approximately the percentage—that is, the percentage share of the local tax revenues in the total of the city revenues and that

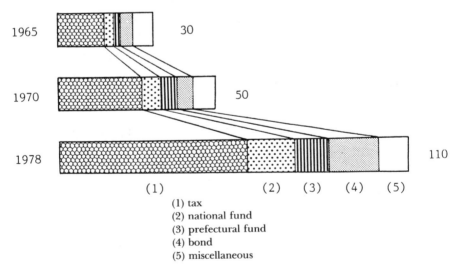

(1) tax
(2) national fund
(3) prefectural fund
(4) bond
(5) miscellaneous

Figure 4.3. *Fiscal revenue per capita (yen 1,000; 1978 price).*

of the inhabitant tax revenue in the total of the local tax revenues were virtually constant at 45 percent. The per capita amount of the local tax increased from Yen 6,900 to Yen 65,000, or by about four times in real terms. In the same period, however, issuance of city bonds gradually increased, with an outstanding amount rising from Yen 700 million to Yen 22,100 million, an increase of thirty times (fifteen times in real terms); the percentage of the redemption for the city bonds rose from 2.8 percent to 8.8 percent of the total city expenditures, thus increasing its reliance on debt (Figure 4.4.).

What should be noted in the process of the urbanization of Machida was the development of disorganized sprawl. Of its 7,154 hectares of city area, the percentage of housing areas increased from only 7 percent in 1960 to 26 percent in 1978, while the percentages of farmland and woodland decreased, respectively, from 40 percent to 21 percent and from 31 percent to 22 percent in the same period. In this process, the housing land areas sprawled at random into farmland and woodland, thus causing more difficulties in the arrangement of essential public facilities. Behind this lay the following causes:

1. Private developers made erratic advance land purchases and housing developments.

2. Even such public developers as the Japan Housing Corporations opted for their housing development projects in cheaper-priced areas, far away from railway stations, with no long-term development plan provided.

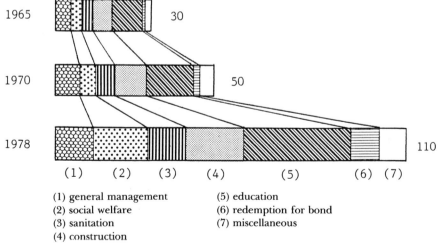

(1) general management	(5) education
(2) social welfare	(6) redemption for bond
(3) sanitation	(7) miscellaneous
(4) construction	

Figure 4.4. *Fiscal expenditure per capita (yen 1,000; 1978 price).*

3. Landowners (farmers), who expected future land price rises, often refused to sell their lands, even after they were surrounded by newly developed housing areas.
4. Neither the central government, Tokyo metropolitan government, nor Machida municipal government could take any effective measure to control the above causes of sprawl.

When the Japan Housing Corporation started land purchases in the city in 1960, the per square meter price of woodland was around Yen 100, and the price of housing land in the city about ten minutes on foot from a railway station was around Yen 1,000, which rose to around Yen 10,000 in 1970 and to around Yen 100,000 in 1980: In other words, the price increased by around 100 times in twenty years. Nonetheless, the increase in the city's real property tax revenues from 1965 to 1978 was by around thirty times from Yen 200 million to Yen 5,800 million.

Along with substantially increased land prices, traditional farmers in the city turned into large income earners, though the acreage in their individual possession originally had been not necessarily large. There are currently around 1,000 farmer households in Machida City, each holding about 1 hectare of farmland and 1 hectare of woodland. Of these, about 200 households include full-time farmers who live in UCAs somwhat away from the town area. Most of these farmers in or near the town area built rental houses or apartment houses to earn household incomes that often by far surpass their incomes from agriculture, as was described in Chapter 3.

The Financial Principle of Suburban Cities

Managing areas adjacent to major cities is very important to the successful management of urban problems. There certainly are many problems in major cities arising from midtown congestion, which, however, can be offset to some extent by convenience. On the other hand, there is virtually no such convenience in the suburban areas due to lack of investment in infrastructure. There certainly are more chances for contact with nature in such suburban areas, but this advantage is also doomed to decrease along with the progress of urbanization. Actually, the green belt between Machida City and the midtown area of Tokyo has gradually eroded as housing development increases. With the completion of the ongoing Tama New Town Development Plan, the Machido will virtually be joined immediately with the midtown area. What methods, then, are available to finance the cost of providing infrastructural conveniences in suburban areas?

It is difficult to have new residents pay all of such cost, since their income level is not high. It might be possible to move the sources of employment together with the population from the midtown area to the suburbs so that they can act as the taxable sources for local governments. However, it is difficult to imagine something like the self-sustained town that the British New Town policy envisaged. Under circumstances of the life-employment scheme that almost all Japanese corporations have adopted, it may be impractical to hope for a company to move its location together with all employees from a major city into a suburban site. It is also unlikely that the new residents in a suburban area can find sufficient employment opportunities in that area.

When it comes to the financial capacity of the so-called parent city—Tokyo in the case of Machida City—financial flexibility is limited as compared to the amount of financial requirements in Machida, since the Tokyo metropolitan government still must allocate vast amounts of funds to advance its midtown redevelopment in order to improve housing facilities in the central area against mishaps such as earthquakes and typhoons.

The task of the central government in this respect is to enhance social overhead capital in rural provinces in order to check the population influx into major cities. If the government neglects this task, suburban investment will increase the number of those seeking opportunities in major cities, thus not helping ease but rather worsening urban problems.

What the central government and the parent city are expected to do is limited by their financial burdens within the framework of the ongoing administrative and financial systems. The primary principle of local finance asks the municipalities to enhance social overhead capital in response to the requirements of urbanization by attaining revenues from taxation on land and buildings within their own jurisdictions. The land and house retention tax (called the rate in Britain and the property tax in the United States) are substantial income sources of the local tax revenues in those two countries. Though the real property tax was created in Japan under the Shoup recommendation after World War II, it could not give full play to its initially expected function because, as was earlier explained, of the exception of farmland on the basis of the 1964 revision to the Supplementary Provisions of the Local Taxes Law and the impractically low standard of land appraisal.

What is needed now is to return to the initial principle. In areas of rapid population increases, an extra amount of cost for infrastructural arrangement would temporarily be required. In such a case, an extraordinary tax can be considered, apart from the general financial requirements, solely to pay this cost. Based on such a concept, the Local Taxes Law allows for the local governments to adopt the city planning tax as a special purpose tax. This city planning tax is levied on land and buildings, with the appraised amount of fixed assets used as its taxable amount. Its rate was raised in 1979 from 0.2 percent to 0.3 percent. What makes this tax different from the real property tax is that it is an earmarked tax with the revenue therefrom appropriated only for city plan works such as roads, parks, and sewage arrangements, while the latter is an ordinary tax with no object of expenditure specified. In other words, since the city planning tax is levied on land and buildings with the revenue therefrom used for infrastructural arrangement, it can help raise the usefulness of land and buildings and as a result the market value thereof. In this sense, this tax functions within the framework of the principle of burden prorated to expected benefit. Not only the city planning tax but also the real property tax play an important role in areas of rapid population increases, since financial requirements increase not only for urban infrastructures but also for other facilities such as compulsory schools.

In reality, however, the revenue from the city planning tax is currently kept at too low a level as compared with the needs of the urban infrastructure. In the case of Machida City, for instance, its revenue from the city planning tax in fiscal year 1977 was only Yen 1,100 million, compared to its appropriation of Yen 3,800 million for the urban infrastructure. I believe it essential to increase the amount of the city planning tax in order to firmly establish the financial foundation of the municipalities in the rapidly population increasing areas.

Some policy instruments control land use, such as zoning by the City Planning Law as well as National Land Use Planning Act. Some schemes expropriate land and raise public funds to provide public facilities, such as Land Readjustment Act and City Planning Tax respectively. These measures are efficient enough for the policy goals, if they are used appropriately. What are lacking are strategies to combine these measures with a will to create and maintain a better environment for people living in urban areas. The key concept of this strategy is to impose stricter controls on landowners' rights to earn gains from and to dispose of land and to ease controls on the rights to use land in urbanization promotion areas.

Notes

1. For comprehensive works on the concept and use of land readjustment, the reader may refer to William A. Doebele, ed., *Land Readjustment: A Different Approach to Financing Urbanization* (Lexington, Mass.: D.C. Heath, 1982), and to Luciano Minerbi et al., *Land Readjustment: The Japanese System* (Honolulu: Department of Urban and Regional Planning, University of Hawaii, 1984).

2. Where the communal contribution rate is $(A - A')/A = \gamma$, and the land price rise rate owing to land readjustment is $(P' - P)/P = \mu$, the expected benefit on the part of a landowner is

$$\mu \geqq \frac{\gamma}{1 - \gamma} \tag{4.1}$$

In other words, a land readjustment project cannot be advantageous to landowners insofar as the land price rise rate after the road construction remains approximately equal to the communal contribution rate. It becomes advantageous to them provided that the land price rises higher than the right side of equation (4.1). For example, given that communal contribution rate is 20 percent, expected land price rise rate μ in a period from the construction start to completion should be 25 percent or higher. Of course, a land readjustment project becomes more favorable to the landowners as the contribution rate becomes smaller and as the land price rise rate becomes higher.

3. Equation (4.1) (see note 2 above) indicated the effect of a land readjustment project in terms of a ratio of land price increase to the prereadjustment land price. However, its interpretation needs modification in the case where the land price rise continues without land readjustment. Provided that the land price rise rate without the effect of land readjustment is μ_1, and the said rate through land readjustment is μ_2, the expression can be rearranged as:

$$\frac{\mu_2}{1 + \mu_1} > \frac{\gamma}{1 - \gamma} \tag{4.2}$$

In other words, the land price rise rate through land readjustment should be discounted by the land price rise rate without it.

Since the land prices in the major urban regions in Japan without land readjustment have been rising at an annual rate of more than 20 percent, $1 + \mu_1$ should reach at least 2, provided that a land readjustment project needs more than four years for completion. With the communal contribution rate assumed at 20 percent as in the case of note 2, these given figures substituted into equation (4.1) produce 0.5. That is, the effect of a land readjustment project in raising the land price should be more than 50 percent.

Though the rate of land price increases through land readjustment was sufficient at 25 percent while land prices were stable, the general land price rises in Japan pressed the required rate up to 50 percent, thus conceivably doubling the difficulty to landowners who participated in a land readjustment project.

On the other hand, even if the expected rate of land price increases through land readjustment is low (e.g., 25 percent), the private space reduction rate should substantially be lowered insofar as land prices continue rising even without land readjustment. The general land price increases obviously strengthen the position of landowners toward the communal contribution under the land readjustment formula.

5

Policies for Land Price Control

Land taxation can directly affect land supply and demand. It was earlier clarified that the inheritance tax is important to farmers in resolving land sales. The real property tax, city planning tax (both of these taxes shall be called land retention tax hereafter because these taxes are levied annually on people who own land) can be interpreted as a kind of annual cost for holding land, a higher rate thereof would decrease the after-tax income on the part of a farmer household, thus leading to its lower living standard. If the householder wants to keep to the same living level or to raise it, he would have to arrange more income sources by selling land either to buy movable assets for more interest income or to build rental houses or apartment houses for more cash income thus increasing land supply. Then, as Figure 3.2. earlier showed in Chapter 3, with the supply curve shifting upward to the right, quantitative expansion of land supply causes the price to fall.

In any taxation on land, the taxable standard and tax rates can legally be revised. Therefore, taxation on land functions to control land price.

Section 1. Land Retention Tax

Disadvantages of the Exception of Farmland from Taxation

The classified lands as the taxable objects for the real property tax and the city planning tax are currently appraised by market value, except farmland, which is still appraised on the basis of the 1963 standard. The 1963 standard was derived from the profitability of the paddyfields on the basis of fiscal year 1961 rice prices. Even at that time, the appraised value of farmland was only one-quarter of its market value, which is no longer justifiable at present after a lapse of twenty years.

With the population of inhabitants having increased against a shortfall of untapped land supply in the UPA in the three major urban regions, land prices rapidly increased, while causing complex social and urban problems. Given this fact, it is evident that the time has come to discontinue the unique exception of farmland from the mechanism of the real property tax.

The appraised price of housing land in Nerima Ward in Tokyo, in the peripheral residential quarter of the city, averages around Yen 200,000 per one tsubo, which is actually too low compared with its market price. While it is permissible to moderate appraisals to some degree, the average amount of farmland in appraisal in the ward is around Yen 200 per one tsubo—only one one-thousandth of the average appraisal of housing land.

As the basic law governing the real property tax and the city planning tax, the Local Taxes Law definitely indicates "the price as of the date of tax assessment" as the standard of land tax. Of course, the rule of the Local Taxes Law is based on the principle of ad valorem or market value taxation, which logically calls for the application of the same appraising method. Granted that agriculture is an industry of relatively low profitability, the price of farmland could reasonably be low, thus leading to a relatively lower tax amount. However, the fact that its market price is rising indicates the possibility of higher profitability by using it for other purposes than agriculture. Therefore, in the light of the principle of equitable taxation, farmland should also be appraised by market value.

In reality, however, as a product of political compromise, a supplementary provision was added to the Local Taxes Law, when it was revised in 1964, to freeze the amount of appraised farmland price at that point in time, and it has remained effective to date. There are discussions on the market value taxation on farmland in UPA to the effect that such taxation aims at driving farmer households out of UPA. This is misinterpretation. The call for equal taxation in UPAs simply aims at a return to the principle.[1]

Effect of the Land Retention Tax

Generally speaking, it is common knowledge that the land retention tax acts as a constant cost for landowners, thus having an effect of increasing land supply. If the value of farmland in the UPA in the three major urban regions had been appraised on the same standard as housing land, the owners of farmland in UPAs would have to pay the land retention tax hundreds to one thousand times the current level because their farmland is appraised at up to one-one thousandth of the appraised value of housing land. To be more specific, in Nerima Ward, though the current amount of the real property tax (including the city planning tax, and this applies elsewhere hereafter) paid by a farmland owner per hectare is around Yen 10,000 a year, it might rise to several hundred million Yen. The farmer households in the UPA in large cities generally have far larger incomes than average workers, since they can earn substantial revenues from the rent of rental houses, apartment houses, and parking lots. Still, if the real property tax would rise to several hundred million Yen for individual landowners, they would have to sell a part of their land.

Increasing the tax would also bring forth substantial tax revenue increases to the financially pinched municipalities in the rapid population increasing areas, thus greatly contributing to the improvement of social overhead capital.

In the described case of Machida City, for instance, its real property tax and city planning tax revenues from land in fiscal year 1977 were, respectively, Yen 3,200 million and Yen 800 million, thus totaling Yen 4,000 million, which was 29 percent of its total tax revenues and 11 percent of the total of its annual revenues. However, the real property tax on farmland in the UPA was—even with the city planning tax revenue added—as low as only Yen 200 million. If farmland plots in the UPA had been appraised—with the exceptional tax measure removed—on a scale equivalent to the average appraisal of housing land (Yen 20,000 per sq m), the appraisal of all these plots would rise to around Yen 200,000 million. With the standard rates of the real property tax and city planning tax levied on this amount, it would add Yen 2,800 million and Yen 600 million, respectively. In other words, the exceptional measure for farmland has deprived Machida City of a potential of Yen 3,400 million. If this amount were added to the city's revenues, its tax revenues total would increase from Yen 14,000 million to Yen 17,000 million.

What should also be noted in this connection is the expected effect of this tax policy in advancing the land readjustment scheme. The main causes of the limited acreage of the land readjustment formula applied areas are attributable to (1) landowners' resistance to the private space reduction system in the formula because of general land price rises and (2) the financial incapacity of local governments to positively advance this formula. However, once the land price rise slows down under the pressure of a higher real property tax rate, they would tend to welcome readjustment since it is a policy instrument to enhance the value of land. At the same time, such a higher tax rate would readily increase the tax revenues on the part of municipalities, thus giving them the capacity to increase appropriations for land readjustment.

*Comments on Arguments against Market-value
Taxation on Farmland*

Though there have been a multitude of criticisms against the policy for
market-value taxation on farmland in UPA, these seemed to have largely
been based on misunderstanding.

One criticism is that market-value taxation on farmland will cause
green plants to vanish from urban areas. However, even without such
taxation, green plants would do so inevitably to some extent in the
course of solving the housing difficulties in the major urban regions,
no matter whether this solution would be by means of the construction
of massive public-operated housing facilities based on housing land
nationalization or of the construction of residential houses for individual
workers based on the financing of required funds at low interest rates
through the housing corporation formula. Any effort to solve the housing problem in the major urban regions without some cost to green-rich
areas will be futile. Even without such taxation, farmers can convert
their farmlands to other uses, and they are actually doing so now.

Here we may call attention to the presence of the Productive Green
Land Law, which was enacted for the purpose of preserving green
farms in the urbanized areas. The law provides for exceptional real
property tax rates on "productive green land" as authorized farms within
the designated area under the City Planning Law.

The exponents of this law emphasized the need of such productive
green land on the grounds that it can act as a refuge place at a time of
emergency, as a buffer against environmental pollution, and as a scenic
attraction and can help secure future public-use land spaces. The first
three are the expected merits of such green land even without the
legislation as long as farmers continue to use it as farmland. However,
farmers might discontinue farming to sell it to a third party. Then,
based on the Public Land Expansion Law, the local government can
exercise its preemption over the green land. However, this option is
nothing more than what can be called a preconsultation with landowners, entitling the municipality to time-limited consultation prior to
any of the third parties, and in case a farmer cannot find an appropriate
buyer within the three-month period, he can transfer the land to a third
party. If the third party does not want to continue farming on the land,
the designation thereof as productive green land would be invalidated
at that time.

Unlike the designation of the UCA, the designation of productive
green land thus involves possibility for invalidation at any time except
when the municipality is prepared to buy it for a park whenever it is
offered for sale. Otherwise, productive green land within the UPA is

insignificant. Once a park space is secured, the productive green land would no longer be needed. If there is any reason to keep a place permanently as a farmland in either an environmental or a landscape aspect, it must be kept so as a part of the park space under the municipality's control.

The question comes down to whether the designation of the productive green land can facilitate the acquisition of a future park space. The main causes of the current difficulty in acquiring public park space can be attributed to the reluctance on the part of farmers to sell land due to the radical land price rises and the financial difficulty on the part of local governments. The designation of a productive green land does not seem to eliminate these causes at all. Insofar as the causes of land price rises to date are left intact, the annual land price rise rate will continue to exceed the annual growth of tax revenues, and this means that even if a future park area is designated as a productive green land, because of the financial difficulty on the part of the local governments, it will become financially more difficult to purchase the area in the future. In a continuously rising market, the local government would have no choice but to give up its preemption right and see the area used for other purposes than a public park.

To make the matters worse, the Productive Green Land Law acts against the said market-value taxation on farmland in UPA, which is essential to get rid of the two causes of difficulty in acquiring public park spaces. In this sense, the law is not only useless but rather detrimental to the acquisition of future park spaces. With respect to an area that should be secured as future park space but would tend to turn into housing land if taxed at market value in the UPA, it should be included in the planned park areas under the City Planning Law. Then, the required fund for purchasing it in the future can be attained from the city planning tax revenue. Supposing that all lands in the UPA are appraised at market value, and the revenue from the city planning tax at a rate of 0.3 percent is totally made available for the acquisition of public park spaces, then 0.3 percent of the total acreage of the UPA can be acquired annually as park spaces. If this system continues for ten years, 3 percent of the acreage of the UPA will become available for park spaces.

In reality, however, the acreage of the designated productive green land is nearly negligible as compared with the total acreage of farmland in the UPA. This fact rather implies that irrespective of the tax rate, farmers prefer to keep themselves free from any restriction in their disposal of farmland at any time.

There is another argument against market-value taxation on farmland in the UPA that such tax policy cannot achieve its objective because the local legislatures are empowered to recycle the revenues from the real property tax to farmers. It is true that as a general practice, they could recycle part or all of the real property tax revenues from farmlands in the UPA to farmers on the basis of their ordinances. Still, it is irrelevant to think that the said policy will bring forth none of its expected effects. As long as the recycled amount of this tax remains insignificant, the local legislatures may be able to continue the makeshift measure. However, once taxation on farmland is made equivalent to housing land, the real property tax revenues from farmlands will conceivably amount to more than 10 percent of all the tax revenues of the local governments. Then, the nonfarming inhabitants would not permit the municipalities to continue recycling the revenues from farmland to a limited number of farmers. In addition, since the revenue of the real property tax is a component of the basic financial revenues of any local government for determining the parity appropriation from the central government to the local government, it seems unlikely that the governments will continue the recycling of the real property tax revenue once it rises to a significant amount.

There is also an argument that market-value taxation on farmland in the UPA will certainly act to increase untapped land supply, but it would not lead to a substantial increase in the supply of newly developed housing land because real estate dealers would buy up the newly supplied untapped lands only to increase their stock. However, unlike the time of the *Building a New Japan* boom, it is no longer easy for them to buy up and keep in stock untapped land in large acreage because of the presence of the special tax on land retention and the heavy tax rate on capital gains from land transfer. In addition, many companies had bitter experiences repaying their huge debts in the recession period following 1973 after having rushed into speculation-based land purchases on borrowings in the boom period. Still, the claimed danger of their buy-up campaign cannot yet be dismissed.

What is basically needed is to expand rapidly the untapped land supply. As Table 3.4. in Chapter 3 earlier showed, the annual total of housing land development was around 500 hectares recently. With no expansion in the acreage of land in stock on the part of developers and dealers taken into account, it can be said that their untapped land purchases would be at most around 1,000 hectares a year. Therefore, even if the housing land developers and real estate dealers start for speculation-based buying up to some extent, around 2,000 hectares of untapped land for annual supply would be sufficient to overwhelm them. What can be proposed in addition on the basis of an assumption that land kept in stock for future sale on the part of developers can be regarded as their raw materials is legislation that limits the permissible maximum of such stock to the quantity equivalent to their actual acreage of housing land supply in a specified preceding period (for example, seven years). Then, if they try to purchase more untapped land along with expansion of untapped land supply, they would be obligated to duly increase their newly developed housing land supply, thus being discouraged from speculation-based purchases. Such a legislation may also preclude nonqualified entrepreneurs from participating in the market of land purchases, thus preventing the once-notorious "land-rolling" transactions in the absence of actual demand. More important, the encouragement of land readjustment will increase housing land supply without intervention by real estate dealers so that their role in the land market can be minimized.

Section 2. Capital Gains Tax

To begin with, it should be noted that any change in the income tax on capital gains would conceivably affect untapped landowners, mostly farmers, in the vicinities of cities and that the main motives of these farmers to sell untapped land are (1) to rebuild their own houses and (2) to build rental houses and apartment houses in order to earn recurrent income. The essential matter of our concern is how the rate of the income tax on capital gains affects farmers' motives for rebuilding their own houses and/or building rental houses and apartment houses as well as the selling acreage of untapped land. We can disregard other income than turnover from land sale and progressiveness of taxation; this means that the tax rates here are proportional on land sales.

The effect of the proportional rate taxation on the income from realized capital gains on the supply of untapped land should be analyzed in two aspects. The one is the impact of any expected change to such tax rates on the current supply of untapped land, and the other is how a tax rate affects the supply of untapped land after it is changed.

Let us begin with the first aspect. If the untapped landowners are informed of forthcoming higher tax rates in the next year, will they increase land sales in the current year while the tax rates are still low? In this case, the supply of untapped land in the current year would increase, and the land price rise would slow down, provided that a majority of untapped landowners think it wise to sell land in the current year. However, this reaction cannot necessarily be counted on. For instance, if they think that the rate of annual price rise next year would be larger than the current year, landowners might think it wise to sell land in the next year even at the cost of higher tax. If they think that the prices will further continue rising even after the next year, they might even think it wise to keep holding their lands for more years until the ripe time for sale comes, irrespective of whether the tax rates will rise. Then, even though the government decides on raising the tax rate beginning with the next year with a view to encouraging the untapped landowners to sell their land within the current year, such a decision may not lead to the expansion of untapped land supply in the current year at all.[2]

Even with the rate hikes of the income tax on capital gains, it still is possible that untapped landowners will delay their land sales. The supply of untapped land decreases, as the untapped landowners slow down their land sales; then the land prices duly turn upward. The actual transition of the housing land supply/demand balances in the major urban regions to date can be said to show that the dominant presence of bullish expectation among untapped landowners about increased land prices has been incorporated into the market forces to cause actual land price rises.

Even in this case, there can be factors that discourage delaying land sales—such as an outlook for the downward turn of land prices, the need on the part of untapped landowners for keeping their household living levels from sinking under the pressure of lower cash incomes or the expansion of cost for continuously holding land. If such factors affect landowners, the tight supply of untapped land would be eased. However, the overwhelming majority of farmers in the vicinities of major cities hold extremely bullish expectations of land price rises. What is more, they are free of the said need for cash income since most of them have access to other income sources such as agriculture and part-time employment and do not have to worry about the cost of holding land as long as the real property tax rate on farmland is kept at the current low level.

With these background factors taken into consideration, it is difficult to predict the effect of a higher rate of income tax on capital gains in increasing land sales ahead of its actual implementation. The only exception is the case where the tax rate is raised up to 100 percent, which I shall refer to later.

If the owners of untapped land expect the future tax rate to come down to below the current rate, they may possibly see more advantage in selling land in the future than selling it under the current rate even in the case where the expected annual land price increase rate is either equivalent to or less than the prevailing interest rate per annum.

The second aspect of a tax rate is how it affects the supply of untapped land after it is lifted.

In this case, the owners of untapped land would see more advantage in selling land at the current stage than in selling it in the future, provided that the expected annual land price rise rate is higher than the prevailing interest rate and that the tax rate is constant. In other words, the given level of tax rate does not directly affect them in determining the time for selling land. Still, the given level of tax rate can to some degree affect the owners of untapped land who have already decided to sell land.

For instance, if the landowner is determined to sell land to gain a certain amount of money to rebuild his own house or to build rental houses or an apartment house, he would have to sell more land if the given tax rate is higher. In this context, a higher tax rate seems to have more effect than a lower tax rate in expediting the supply of untapped land.

However, the income tax on capital gains, if its rate is extremely high, would have an adverse psychological effect on the owners of untapped land, offsetting the above effect to some extent. That is, they would expect further land price rises as well as a possibility for downward revision of the ongoing tax rate. Even if the rate of the income tax on capital gains is set at an extremely high level, many of the owners of untapped land would reasonably think about the possibility of tax rate reductions some time in the near future, since they know that the land tax system has been revised almost yearly. They may judge it advantageous to wait for the time when the high tax rate comes down to a reasonable level, even though the expected rate of annual land price rise by that time might be lower than the prevailing interest rate. In other words, they may opt for holding land until their selling opportunity comes. I would like to call this kind of behavior institutional speculation because its outcomes resemble those of market speculation. In this sense, it can be said that even if a high tax rate on capital gains from land sales is institutionally kept at a given level, the high rate itself acts as an obstacle to the supply of untapped land insofar as the owners of untapped land can look forward to the possibility of it coming down to a lower level in the future.

Such propensity of landowners is significant, especially with respect to the calls for 100 percent taxation on capital gains from land. The apostles of 100 percent taxation believe that if the expected future gains from land sales is nullified under the 100 percent rate of tax, the owners of untapped land would no longer wait for the future and would immediately start selling their land. Among a large number of landowners might be those who would act as predicted. However, there also are those who would rather give up the intention of selling land if the planned land sales bring no profit at all to them (especially among the landed farmers who are free of the need for cash income to pay living expenses). In my observations, the landowners in the second group overwhelm in number those in the first. Thus, even though a limited number of the owners of untapped land might sell land, what they can add to the untapped land market as a whole would be not substantial as long as the rest of such owners remain holding their land.

If the 100 percent tax rate is maintained on capital gains from land, there could even be the danger of widespread tricky tax evasion practices. Any expected effect of taxation should be examined in the light of tax collectability.

A too high rate of the income tax on capital gains causes the danger of discouraging land supply, and a too low rate fails to achieve the expected effect of its role in income redistribution. In addition, frequent rate variation either upward or downward leads the owners of untapped land into speculation about future rate changes. In other words, such a tax rate should be maintained at a level neither too high nor too low (for instance, 40 percent) over a long period. However, the income tax on capital gains itself cannot urge the owners of untapped land to sell land as long as they can expect larger annual land price increases than the annual interest rate.

Finance specialists tend to regard the tax system as a component of policy-mix in macroeconomic context and are reluctant to change tax schemes in order to implement a narrowly addressed political goal because it, according to their opinion, may disturb the optimal resource allocation. The present tax schemes are, in many cases, outcomes of repeated compromises that have been made after struggles among interested parties. Property taxation based on market-value assessment is a solution that realizes the optimal resource allocation while maintaining neutrality in income distribution. Proportional rate taxation on capital gains from land disposal is a solution that minimizes the adverse effect of institutional speculation.

Notes

1. Some readers might find a trace of Henry George's single tax theory in the prescribed policy approach for repressing land prices by higher land retention tax. However, since I believe that the modern tax system should be established with progressive-rate income tax as its core, I cannot support the single tax theory, which was based on land retention tax, while dismissing the other taxes as unessential. In addition, I should note here that I do not think that land problems, especially land problems in major cities, alone represent all the problems in Japan at present. My position is that provided that there is an available measure to solve any given specific problem, such a measure should be applied to solve the problem separate from the whole of the issue that comprises it, insofar as the given circumstances permit such an approach.

   Nevertheless I certainly sympathize with George, who wrote *Progress and Poverty with Reference to the Realities in the United States in the Latter Half of the Nineteenth Century.* The U.S. situation at that time (workers lived a hand-to-mouth existence despite great expansion in production, and speculators dominated the great West and overshadowed the hope for the frontier) may have given rise to his thoughts. I wonder if the situation in major cities in Japan today is not very similar to the background of his thought. Despite the leap forward in the growth of production, which, however, has led to no substantial change in labor's relative share of wealth, workers cannot improve their poor housing situations because of rampant speculative transactions in land (to increase land in stock on expectation for future land price rises). I believe that George deserves much higher appreciation today.

2. Where the current land price is Yo and tax rate to, let us assume that a landowner anticipates that n years later the land price and tax rate will be, respectively, Yn and tn. Then, if the discount rate to convert the expected land price n years later to the price at the current stage is ρ (the term *interest rate* can also be used, without causing misunderstanding, as representing the maximum of the expected earning rates on other assets), and if the price fluctuations as well as the recurrent expenditures and outlays on land and the land acquisition cost are regarded as negligible, the conditions for selling land at the current stage in better economic advantage than n years later can be expressed as:

$$(1 - \text{to}) \text{ Yo} > (1 - \text{tn}) \hat{\text{Y}}\text{n}/(1 + \rho)^n \qquad (5.1)$$

(ˆ herein shows the variable as expected value.)

The left side of equation (5.1) shows the after-tax proceeds from a land sale at the current stage, and the right side shows the expected amount of the after-tax proceeds from a land sale n years later, which is discounted by the earning ratio of other assets into its expected value at the current stage. The sign of inequality indicates that the land sale at the current stage brings forth more returns. This expression can be rearranged as:

$$\hat{\text{Y}}\text{n} < (1 + \rho)^n \text{ Yo } (1 - \text{to})/(1 - \text{tn}) \qquad (5.2)$$

For direct comparison of Yn and Yo, the expected value of the annual land price rise rate is shown as r and Yn is substituted with $(1 + r)$ Yo; then, the following expression is obtained:

$$\hat{r} < \sqrt[n]{\frac{1 - \text{to}}{1 - \text{tn}}} \ (1 + \rho) - 1 \qquad (5.3)$$

What this expression means is that it brings fewer proceeds to sell land n years later than to sell it at the current stage provided that the tax rate n years later is tn. In other words, it indicates both the maximum value of the expected land price rise rate for selling land and the minimum thereof against selling land. If the expected land price rise rate is smaller than the right side, it is wise to sell land immediately; otherwise, it is wise not to do so.

The above expression can also give a tax rate tn that makes land sale at the current stage more advantageous than n years later, provided that to and ρ are the given conditions and that the expected value of the future land price rise rate is $\hat{r}$.

However, what can be derived from equation (5.2) is that it is only conditionally applicable—that is, if tax rate tn is made larger, the right side of equation (5.2) would become larger, but this right side can be made as close to discount rate ρ as you may want to by making n larger to postpone the selling time. In other words, no matter how high a tax rate (provided that it does not exceed 1) the government may adopt, the landowners can act against it by postponing the selling timepoint, thus resultantly nullifying the expected effects of the government's policy of expediting land supply.

For example, with the current tax rate, the tax rate one year later and the interest rate, respectively, given at 0 percent, 20 percent, and 10 percent, the right side of equation (5.2) makes 0.375, thus indicating that land sale one year later is more advantageous than at present insofar as the land price rise rate is larger than 37.5 percent. However, if the expected land price rise rate is smaller, such as 25 percent, land sale at present is more advantageous than one year later. Even in this case, however, provided that the tax rate is pegged to the same level after its initial rise, the right side becomes 0.23, with n given 2, thus indicating that to sell land two years later is more advantageous than to sell it at present. In order to let the landowners sell land immediately instead of two years later in the case where the expected land price rise rate is 25 percent, the tax rate two years later should be set at 25 percent instead of 20 percent (then, the right side becomes 0.27, thus exceeding 0.25). Even so, if the landowners postpone land sale to three years later, instead of two years later, the right side becomes 0.21, thus indicating that even under the condition of the expected land price rise rate at 25 percent, it is disadvantageous to sell land immediately.

Even if the tax rate shall be raised to 75 percent (the current maximum of the inheritance tax rate) next year, the landowners can expect more advantage by delaying the land sale eight more years than selling it now, provided that the expected land price rise rate and the current tax rate are, respectively, 25 percent.

6

A Proposal for an Integrated Land Policy

Earlier chapters have repeatedly stressed the need to combine policy instruments. This chapter presents a proposal for integrating several policy instruments in order to implement the goals of land policy that were stated in the previous chapters. It is crucial for us to understand that there is an effective and viable land policy so that people can abandon the myth of the futility of land policy and begin to study the actual causes for their land and housing difficulties.

Section 1. A Comprehensive Land Policy for Housing Development

Interaction Between Policy Instruments

This discussion has focused on determining the most effective land policy for achieving a given objective. In reality, however, policy is often given multidimensional objectives, and a policy instrument that can effectively serve a certain given objective at times causes adverse effects to another objective. For instance, if a UPA is made too small because of precautions against the danger of sprawl, that would accordingly limit housing land supply and might fail to achieve the objective of curbing land price rises.

At times, however, different policy instruments can supplement each other through interaction, thus mutually helping the other achieve its objective. For instance, a high city planning tax in the UPA will make it easier to distinguish the UPA from the UCA, and such distinction in turn offers the legal basis for imposition of the city planning tax as a special purpose tax.

To begin with, what was essential at the time of the revision of the

City Planning Law was to integrate UPA zoning and market value taxation on farmland in the UPA. Then Minister of Construction Shigeru Hori decided to eliminate the strong pressure exerted by farmers' organizations. This error led to the rise of high expectations among farmers for inclusion of their lands into the UPA, without high taxation and with the possibility for land conversion at any time, and the unnecessary expansion of the UPA over to areas that were unlikely to be urbanized in the near future. Because of this error, market value taxation on farmland in the UPA became in turn more difficult. The discussion that separated the two policy instruments, though these were the integral components of land policy, can be registered as one of the gross errors in the postwar history of internal administration.

A Proposal on Land Policy

Let me propose here a land policy that targets the following three points:

Target One is to lower the land price—to halve the current price level (down to around Yen 50,000 per sq m in the suburbs in and around Tokyo).

Target Two is to expand housing in stock—to allow every household to acquire its residential house with one room per family member.

Target Three is to improve the housing environment—in ten years' time, to arrange towns that are one hour by train for commuters from the city center with city water and sewage service systems completed and with public spaces, including parks and streets, provided at an acreage of no less than 30 percent in all housing areas.

Of course, there can be more targets than these three for land policy; however, I believe these three are most important. I believe that the following three policy approaches are essential to achieve these policy targets:

1. Implementation of the market-value taxation on farmland in the UPA within the major urban regions;
2. Higher city planning tax rate—it should be raised from current 0.3 percent to at least 1.0 percent;
3. Promotion of land readjustment by the local governments and more subsidization on the part of the central government, even if the acreage of those projects and necessary appropriation thereby would increase.

With farmland in the UPA appraised on a scale equivalent to housing land, the farmland owners therein each would have to pay a significant amount of the real property tax and the city planning tax every year, thus, as I described earlier, leading to more supply of untapped land and then to repressed land prices.

Currently, the tax assessment standard on farmland in the UPA in major cities are one-several hundredth as compared with the tax assessment standard of nearby housing land plots. If this standard is raised to a level equivalent to the standard for housing land, most of the farmland owners would have to pay taxes every year beyond their agricultural income from their farms. For instance, the average annual earning from rice paddyfield per hectare is around Yen 400,000. However, if the paddyfield is appraised at Yen 10,000 per sq m, the per hectare amount of tax payments for holding the land would reach as much as Yen 2,400,000, with the real property tax at the rate of 1.4 percent and the city planning tax at a rate raised to 1.0 percent levied. What should also be noted is that the more intense the sprawl is in the UPA, the more deserted would be farmland therein in correspondence to its higher land price. Therefore, with the said measures implemented, the difference between agricultural earnings and the amount of tax levies would become larger, thus compelling farmers to sell their lands part by part.

If a farmer intends to limit land sales in order only to earn cash for paying tax on the whole of his land, the part for sale would be 2.4 percent of his land a year, since the annual sum rate of the real property tax and the city planning tax is 2.4 percent. If he intends to make a deposit with a bank to earn sufficient interest payment to pay the annual tax on his remaining land, he would have to sell at least one-quarter of his currently owned land and invest at an interest rate of 6 percent per annum.

Of a total of farmland in the UPA in Tokyo and the three adjacent prefectures at around 60,000 hectares, only less than 2 percent of it is annually converted into housing land. With this farmland taxed equivalent to housing land, the estimated supply increment would be 2.4 percent of the total acreage even in a conservative estimate, which is more than equal to the current quantitative supply. With the quantitative supply of untapped land doubled, the land price will obviously fall, provided that there is no change in demand.

The land readjustment project is a policy instrument to arrange public-use spaces through a contribution of private spaces, thus leading to the achievement of the third policy target aiming at securing public spaces of no less than 30 percent. Even though the contribution ratio were kept down to 20 percent, this target would possibly be achieved, since around 10 percent of public-use spaces such as streets and waterways normally preexist in the land readjustment area even before the implementation of the readjustment project. Therefore, even under the condition of 20 percent contribution of private space, landowners can expect to have 80 percent of their land turned into housing land plots in good quality, with the readjustment and development costs fully covered at the expense of the local governments.

What benefits would a land readjustment project bring to the local government? As was mentioned in the case of housing land development by private developers, the construction cost per square meter at Yen 20,000 can produce well-arranged public facilities, including city water and sewage service facilities as well as streets and park. Given the share for public spaces at 30 percent of the total area, the per square meter cost would rise to around Yen 30,000. Provided that the central government subsidizes half of the cost, what remains is Yen 15,000 of the cost on the part of the local government.

The local government may initially pay this cost by issuing bonds. Provided that the interest rate on this bond is 7 percent per annum, the interest payment per square meter a year is Yen 1,050. However, the per square meter tax revenue from the land that has been well facilitated with roads and others would be Yen 1,200, if the land is appraised at Yen 50,000 per square meter, and this per square meter tax revenue is sufficient for the required amount to pay the per square meter interest rate on the outstanding bond.

What remains is the redemption of the principal of the outstanding bond, which will be left to local government. Currently, the Ministry of Finance's fund, based on the postal money deposits as the fund source, accepts local bonds extensively for city water and sewage service works on the condition that the principal be redeemable in thirty-five years after a period of deferment for five years. With this system applied to the land readjustment project, the local government can plan to repay the debt of Yen 15,000 per square meter over a period of forty years. The local government can repay the debt with the future increase of the residential tax of the newly settled population in the developed areas.

In fact, I described the above procedure backwards. In order to achieve the policy target of developing well-arranged housing areas, each provided with a total of public spaces at 30 percent or more—involving water, sewage service, and other public facilities—at a price of Yen 50,000 per square meter, one-half of subsidization from the central government for municipal land readjustment projects and authorization for the local governments to issue their bonds for their promotion of land readjustment projects are indispensable.

Compared with the housing land development projects by private developers, the land readjustment approach can offer housing land to users at cheaper cost. In the case of housing land development, for instance, by a private developer, approximately one-third of the development cost is the required interest payment on his borrowings in the period from the acquisition of land to the sale of newly developed land; such interest payment during the construction period is much less in the case of land readjustment because the land readjustment requires no land acquisition cost.

The prescribed policy instruments are feasible. I believe that there can be other sets of such or different instruments. However, the prescribed measures will be sufficient to establish an effective and viable land policy.

Even in the Tokyo Region where the housing situation is believed to be most stringent in Japan, conditions will permit the achievement of the prescribed targets. Such conditions existed even ten years ago. With the income level expected to annually rise, it was generally accepted that as long as land prices are pegged to the same level, the housing problem would be solved as time rolls on along with the annual rise of personal income. However, the substantial rise in income levels that occurred in the past can no longer be expected today. Since the current land price is far beyond the reach of consumers at large, merely pegging it to the current level cannot solve the housing problem. Since it is essential to lower the land price level in absolute terms, policy measures should be more radical than they were ten years ago.

It is widely recognized even within the government authorities that a strong land policy and market value taxation on farmland in the UPA will be certainly effective in substantially increasing untapped land supply, thus functioning to stabilize housing land prices. Nonetheless, this policy has not been brought to the working stage because of objections made by politicians who fear losing farmers' ballots in urban electoral districts. Needless to say, protecting the benefits of a small group at the cost of the interests of a large majority runs counter to the principle of the constitution and betrays political ethics. What should be noted in particular is that being aware of the effects of the market value taxation on farmland in the UPA, the opposition parties, which self-style themselves as acting in the interests of the workers, still oppose this policy only in an attempt to curry favor with farmers in the major urban regions (most of these farmers do not support the opposition parties), thus shamelessly neglecting the national aspect of their political responsibilities.

Social Significance of Land Policy

The prescribed policy targets will lead to the realization of aspirations among people who still live in tiny flats in small wooden apartment houses and continue to save in the hope of purchasing their own houses some time in the future. Suppose that land prices fall to the level of ten years ago; the price of a housing land plot in a suburban town about one hour by train from the city center would be around Yen 50,000 per sq m. Then, the price of a 200 sq m lot would be Yen 10 million. With an average-level house of 100 sq m built—which may be around Yen 8 million unless one wants an extravagant house—built in this lot, the total cost would be around Yen 18 million.

Take the household of a worker, for instance, in his mid-thirties with two children in the third income bracket by the quintile income classification. His annual income was Yen 3.5 million, and the sum of his savings was around Yen 6 million, according to the 1977 statistics. With the loan of Yen 12 million from the Housing Loan Corporation added to the savings, he can acquire the prescribed house, provided that his monthly payment on loan is around Yen 60,000 (which makes annual installments at around Yen 700,000, which is around 20 percent of his annual income and within his repayment capacity).

This calculation was made backwards. For the purpose of ensuring that the above-average worker household can pay for a housing land lot with its own house, the amount of the loan should be limited to Yen 8 million. With the sum of his savings added to this, the total was broken down into the housing cost and land cost, which led to the price of Yen 50,000 per sq m for a proper size of lot at a place about one hour by train for commuters to the city center.

The prescribed targets will be more welcomed by those who are looking for available rental houses or apartment flats than acquiring their own houses. The current rents for the flats in public-built condominium apartment houses normally include by more than 50 percent the cost for repaying the principal of fund used for the acquisition cost. If the land price can be cut back down to half of the current level, these rents would be lowered by at least 25 percent. There are, of course, cheaper public-built apartment houses that were built long ago when land prices and the construction costs were much lower, but the rents for flats in such apartment houses have recently been rising to maintain balance with the rents at the newly built condominium houses. If the rents at the newly built condominium houses could be kept lower, the flat rents at the old apartment houses would not rise as high as now, thus affecting downward the rents at privately owned apartment houses.

Then, what would be the impact of a land price fall on those who already own their houses? For the persons who acquired their houses more than ten years ago, the land price fall to a level ten years ago causes no actual loss. It is true that the market value of their housing land lots as property will certainly decline, but it would cause no difficulty or damage to their daily use of land, insofar as their lots are used only for housing purpose. On the other hand, the land price fall would mean lower inheritance tax payments.

A land price decrease, however, would cause a problem to those who acquired their own houses in the past ten years especially in the case of those who owned houses at the cost of bank loans, since such a price fall will in no way help decrease the future amount of their repayment. Even in this case, however, there will be no physical loss to their lots and houses. In the worst case, they can still sell the mortgaged land and house to buy a new house at some other place with a new loan.

However, when it comes to landed farmers in the UPA the story is different. To these people, the land price fall means a devaluation of property and loss in expected profit, which, however, is not an actual loss of profit. In addition, they may have already achieved windfall profit, albeit by varying degrees, by selling their lands in the past ten years. This explains why farmers are expected to bear the burden resulting from a land price fall.

How much would the price of untapped land be if newly developed housing land should be priced at Yen 50,000 per sq m? On the preconditions that all the construction cost be, as prescribed, covered with the appropriations from public funds and that the public space rate under the Land Readjustment Scheme is set at 30 percent, the price of untapped land should be Yen 15,000 per sq m or less. If around 10 percent of the land readjustment area is already occupied with such public spaces as interfarm lanes and waterways prior to housing land development, Yen 17,000 would be payable for untapped land per sq m, which, however, is less than one-fifth of the current untapped land price. Still, this price is sufficiently higher than the average price for paddyfields in the agricultural areas, which is Yen 10 million per hectare or Yen 1,000 per sq m, and is far above its estimated capital value at Yen 5 million per hectare, if calculated on the basis of the profitability of average paddyfields when used for cropping. In other words, even if the untapped land price comes down to Yen 17,000 per sq m, farmers in the UPA would still be able to expect more profit from land sales compared to farmers in rural agricultural areas.

Farmers in areas other than the major metropolitan regions would welcome the policy because along with progress of the conversion of farmland into housing land in the major city regions, there would be more allowance on the national level for the policy-based crop diversion from rice and more urban markets for their dry field products. (With a view to minimizing rice production surplus, the Ministry of Agriculture, Forestry, and Fishery is advancing a policy of encouraging farmers to divert rice growing to other crops.) In fact, the farmers in the UPA in major city regions who continue insignificantly profitable urban agriculture without converting land to more profitable rental houses can be said to be depriving rural farmers, who have no other significant income opportunities than agriculture, of the opportunity and market for increased income. In this respect, such an organization of farmers as the Central Union of Agricultural Cooperations Associations should be criticized for opposing the market value taxation on farmland in the UPA as diverging from the requirements of its Charter of Incorporation.

Private firms holding real estate will never welcome the prescribed policy measures, including those for repressing land prices, since these will deal a serious blow to the companies—no matter whether housing land developers or others—which still hold in stock large acreages of land they bought some time ago on the expectation of future land price rises. In the case of housing land developers in particular, they will be deprived of a major profit opportunity when the land development works are placed under the Land Readjustment Scheme. What will be left to them will be mainly planning, designing, and civil engineering, with access to land purchase and sale virtually becoming impossible.

It is obvious that strong land policy causes disadvantages for private capital. Notwithstanding, the prescribed land policy measures may bring forth benefits to capital as a whole. For instance, with the land price rises stopping, it will become easier for companies to acquire essential industrial and commercial sites for their business activities, thus facilitating the expansion of productive activities. In addition, well-arranged urban development without the barrier of land price increases will not only reduce the social cost, for which individual firms are partly accountable, but also help raise labor productivity by decreasing the waste of manpower in commuting during rush hour traffic congestion.

Therefore, if the conservative political forces become aware of the need for protecting and acting in the interests of capital as a whole on the basis of growing public awareness of the importance of such interests ahead of the interests of specific capital, even the conservative government will have to adopt a land policy of repressing land price rise. Because of the position of the working class toward this issue, a large majority of the capitalist class may have no choice but to yield to its decision.

In this event, the attitude of financial capital is especially important. Land has to date been the most reliable collateral security for loans because its annual price rise has exceeded the interest rate. If the land price stops rising or even starts falling, land as such security will radically be devalued and will raise doubts about the reliability of secured land for outstanding loans. Therefore, financial capital by itself alone will never positively support any policy that may function to repress land price. Since the development of the postwar Japanese economy has been achieved structurally on the basis of the selective financing formula, the attitude of financial institutions may definitely affect the attitude of the entire capitalist class. On the other hand, because of the importance of the position of financial capital in the Japanese economy, it may have to act—no matter whether it likes to do so or not—along with the common interests of the total capital.

The current situation in Japan can be said to involve some psychological elements leading to totalitarianism. It is said that 90 percent of the Japanese people identify themselves as the middle class. If their psychological position as the middle class starts crumbling with no hope for further income rise—especially if they find it difficult to carry their schedule for repaying the housing loans on the basis of expected annual income rises, or if they find money saving efforts futile against the skyrocketing land prices despite lowered interest rates—their distrust of politics could rapidly increase. Rightists could organize the dissatisfied masses into a political force, while the left-wing reformists repeat their internal strife among one another.

Section 2. The Broadening Perspective of Land Policy

This book has examined the feasibility of policy for repressing housing land prices in order to solve the housing problem in major cities. No matter how important this problem is, it is a mere fragment of the massive problems with which we are faced today. The land problem in major cities is a part of a more important issue at least in two aspects. First of all, in achieving better land utilization on the national level, the most important task is to plan the relocation of industry and population with a view to realizing the ideal utilization and preservation of national land. The problem of land use in major cities is only a component of this issue equal with such requirements as forestry maintenance, farmland productivity, industrial plant siting, arrangement of truck transportation routes, seashore protection, and preservation of historical and scenic sites. The most important factor of the metropolitan problem is to improve living and housing environments in large cities. The housing problem is only a component of this issue, together with such problems as urban environmental pollution, urban transportation, and urban crimes.

One should not forget the forest for the trees. Experienced professors usually advise students that they must start studying a given theme as a part of a major issue after correctly determining its position within the framework of the whole. While advancing the study, they must constantly pay attention to its correlation with the whole. I dared to run counter to this common sense and analyzed the fragment apart from the whole. Generally speaking, such an approach is liable to error. This chapter broadens its perspective hereafter and analyzes some factors that have not been referred to in the previous chapters and sections.

Improvement of the Housing Situation and Population Transfer

This book proposes policy measures for creating conditions that may improve the housing situation in Japan. Whether or not the proposed policy measures will succeed depends on the merits of each chapter. However, even though the individual objectives are fulfilled to a satisfactory degree, it would become necessary to carefully review the main objective itself. If the policy has resulted in expediting the population inflow into major cities, it would only be more difficult to establish a plan for land use throughout the country or further worsen environment in major cities.

To state the conclusion first, the improvement of the housing situation in major cities (including per capita floor space, washroom and kitchen and other utilities, environmental conditions such as sunshine and ventilation, as well as economic costs such as rent and housing acquisition costs) is unlikely to expedite the inflow of population into major cities. Various survey results to date (one of which I referred to in Chapter 3), indicate that the main causes of the concentration of population into major cities are readily available employment opportunities and higher-learning opportunities.

It may be true that the poor housing situation in major cities acts as a negative factor to the concentration of population in major cities. Yet this does not mean that improvement of the housing situation in major cities will infallibly expedite population inflow. What matters is the method of improving the housing situation there. Let us suppose an extreme case where a large number of public housing buildings are built with rents subsidized from public funds only in major cities. Then, the inflow of population into such cities would be expedited. However, in fact, there is no likelihood for such biased allocation of public funds to a limited number of major cities. On the other hand, even in the case where the land prices in major cities are repressed by means of the prescribed tax intervention in land market, it is as yet unlikely that the land prices in the major metropolitan regions would become cheaper than in rural areas, unless a radical change occurs in the pattern of interregional distribution of employment opportunity. Since a decline of land prices in major cities will be followed by a due decline of rural land prices by means that are adopted in major cities, if the housing situation in major cities is improved, the rural housing situation would conceivably also be improved.

Granted that the poor housing situation in major cities is playing a role in discouraging the population inflow to some extent, it is absurd to neglect efforts to improve the urban housing situation. This approach is tantamount to saying that the increasing environmental pollution in major cities should be left intact, since it will discourage the population inflow into urban areas.

Of course, policy for deconcentrating population as well as deconcentrating employment opportunities and higher-learning opportunities is welcome. However, this position does not contradict the need for emphasis on improving the housing situation.

Improvement of Land Use

Since improvement of the urban housing situation would not act to expedite substantially the population inflow into major cities, it may conceivably cause no serious impact on other urban problems such as environmental pollution. If any serious problem occurs, it would be in association with the methods applied for improving the housing situation. This section analyzes the problem of small houses in congestion and the problem of chaotic coexistence of factories and residential houses with a view to determining whether the prescribed land policy measures, given some extent of success, would cause any detrimental effect on these.

The so-called miniplot development has recently turned into a new problem. However, given the fact that the miniplot users had no other choice but to buy small housing plots because of high land prices, it is obvious that this problem would easily be solved once the policy to repress land prices succeeds. A more important problem is the impact of this policy on the shabby wooden apartment houses spreading along the Yamate Loop Line in Tokyo. Because most of these apartment houses were built in the late 1950s or early 1960s, they are not only qualitatively inferior and obsolete but also are vulnerable to fire and other mishaps because of their congested siting and inferior sunshine and ventilation conditions. It is said that once a big earthquake strikes the Tokyo Region, the wooden apartment houses in congested areas would be most seriously damaged. One of the important tasks in coping with the problems of major urban areas is to get rid of such apartment houses. The most effective way to solve this is to convert these apartment houses into medium- and high-rise incombustible housing buildings. Though it is generally understood that the high-density urban redevelopment is required to intensify the utilization density of urban land space, more consideration should be given when redeveloping such areas to converting the wooden houses into incombustible buildings and to securing sufficient public spaces such as parks and streets. In this connection, these buildings need not be high-rise buildings, which often lose broken windows during big earthquakes. It is more desirable to convert the wooden apartment houses into medium-rise fireproof buildings of four or five stories.

Even after these areas are redeveloped, the population density per unit of housing land space would make no substantial difference from the pre-redevelopment density, if the redevelopment creates necessary and sufficient public space and provide medium-rise housing buildings. Therefore, in order to provide larger housing floor space per person through the redevelopment, it will be necessary to move a part of inhabitants to the suburban areas, thus requiring the construction of more houses in the suburbs. After all, the policy for lowering housing land prices will not directly contribute to the promotion of urban redevelopment. Indirectly, however, the substantial increase in housing supply in the suburban areas will have some effect on facilitating the promotion of urban redevelopment through relative decline in demand for wooden apartment houses in the city center by attracting a part of the current inhabitants of such apartment houses into the suburbs.

Next is the problem of the chaotic coexistence of factories and residential houses. Most important in connection with this problem is environmental pollution such as noise, vibration, offensive smell, air pollution, and water pollution originating from factories. These nuisances should be prevented by the factories, and this should be emphasized time and again. The improvement of the housing situation and the prevention of environmental pollution are two separate objectives that can be achieved by means of separate policy approaches, and these do not interfere with each other. In principle, however, it is preferable to avoid the coexistence of factories and residential houses, since it is technically difficult to completely terminate the emission of pollutants and hazards from industrial facilities no matter how strict the environmental controls may be, let alone commonplace hazards that the incoming and outgoing trucks at factories cause to inhabitants and the danger of explosives and/or inflammables stored at such facilities that might blast at any time.

However, as is evident from the process of such mixed coexistence of factories and residential houses, residential houses usually intrude on vacant spaces among the previously sited industrial facilities. There-fore, in order to prevent the mixed coexistence of industrial facilities and residential houses, it is essential to enforce a land use control system so that industrial siting can be limited only within the specific areas, with the building of residential houses prohibited even in the peripheries of such areas. In reality, however, landowners usually strongly react against the enforcement of such control (to be specific, the designation of the exclusive industrial area under the City Planning Law) on private land against the building of residential houses on private land for the reason that it would lead to lower land prices (residential land prices are much higher than industrial land prices). What generally occurred, as a compromise, has been in many instances the designation of the areas as the quasi-industrial areas, where both of the industrial siting and the building of residential houses are permitted.

In this respect, there are two approaches to a solution. The one is to arrange strict control over each factory sited in the quasi-industrial area with respect to the building-to-lot ratio and the distance between the lot boundary and the building so that a buffer zone can be installed at the factory's cost to keep residential houses away from it. With this control implemented, it would become virtually impossible for industrial facilities to site themselves at the high-priced locations in the major metropolitan regions because they would have to purchase much larger plots than they are currently required to own. The second approach is to designate the areas that the public organizations acquired for develop-ment or reclaimed and developed as the exclusive industrial areas so that industrial siting can be limited within these areas.

The said policy approaches are possible even in the current situation but will be more effective once it becomes feasible—with the land prices repressed in the peripheries of major cities—for industrial facilities and public organizations to acquire the land plots they need, including the required buffer zones. In this sense, it can be said that the policy for repressing land prices will help avoid the chaotic coexistence of factories and residential houses. In addition, once land prices are actually brought down, the designation of the exclusive industrial area would more easily be applied to private land than now because landowners would weaken their currently strong opposition to such action.

Though these measures may effectively function to prevent residential houses from mingling with industrial facilities in the future, they cannot immediately sweep away the existing mixture of factories and residential houses. What should be done to eliminate the existing mixture is to make painstaking efforts along the current policy line for moving indus-trial facilities out of the urban centers to rural sites with the evacuated sites used as parks or for the redevelopment of the wooden apartment houses in congested areas. I believe it necessary to separate the policy toward the existing poor conditions that have been born out of the past from the policy for preventing the rise of such conditions in the future.

Improvement of the housing situation by repressing the land prices will, as I described, not stimulate the population influx into major cities and, consequently, will involve no substantial possibility of further worsening the urban problems such as city pollution and disasters. Of course, it is undeniable that the rise of massive new residential houses in suburban areas under this policy will lead to growth of requirements for various public facilities, thus raising new problems if no adequate method is available for covering the new financial cost to meet the new requirements. The suburban areas are basically expected to bear the substantial part of the financial cost to meet the new local requirements, though the central government and the parent cities may also bear their shares to some extent. Of course, the new residents must share in the local financial cost, but their income level is generally not sufficiently high to cover all the cost. The balance should be covered by the persons who have gained from the local land price rises and are likely to continuously enjoy such gains for the future. I presented a detailed discussion of this point in Chapters 4 and 5.

Relationship with Nationwide Land Use

Let me next take a look at the possible impact of the improved housing situation in major cities on land use on the national level. As was described earlier, improvement of the housing situation in major cities has little possibility of expediting the inflow of population into these cities but will inevitably erode parts of farmland and woodland in the process of massive housing land development in the suburban areas. In other words, it will indisputably affect nationwide land use to some degree; the question is to what extent it will do so.

Let me assume that all the farmlands in the UPA in the three major metropolitan regions with Tokyo, Osaka, and Nagoya as their cores will be converted into urban use. The total of such farmlands is 140,000 hectares (this area is enough to improve the housing situation in major cities), and 2.5 percent of the total farmland acreage in Japan, which is 5.5 million hectares. Even if all of 140,000 hectares of farmland is converted into other uses, I do not think that this conversion would immediately worsen the food balance in Japan, since this country is suffering from surplus production of rice and the total area of paddyfields subject to the policy for diversion from rice to other crops is as large as 400,000 hectares. If all the paddyfields in the UPA in major city areas are made convertible into other uses on the priority basis, the required acreage for crop diversion from rice in rural areas would accordingly decrease.

Farmlands in the UPA are currently the supply sources of fresh vegetables for urban markets that are superior in freshness to those sent from distant sources. However, even if all the farmlands in the UPA disappear, farmlands in such hinterlands of major cities as the UCA would start supplying their citizens with fresh vegetables. It is unlikely that there can be any substantial difference in freshness between vegetables produced in farmlands in the UPA, which are within 30 km from the urban center, and those produced in the UCA, which spread along a circle about 50 km from the urban center. In short, suburban farmlands will inevitably disappear to some extent in the process of improving the housing situation in major cities but certainly not to the extent that may cause a serious damage to domestic agricultural production as a whole. If Japanese agriculture is really in a critical situation, as some claim, agricultural administration as a whole has failed to overcome the historical weakness of Japanese agriculture based on minor farm operation and to attain farmers' trust. Attributing its cause only to the urbanization of the major city regions is trying to pass the responsibility to a third party. The same can also be said about woodland.

Some sources claim that farmland and woodland, not as lands of production but as open spaces, are essential in the major city regions. This is true. The green-rich open spaces not only offer areas of recreation for urban citizens who lead a hectic life but also can act to help refresh the urban environment and as refuge areas during emergencies. Eliminating such important open spaces by improving the housing situation in major cities would cause serious problems. Urbanization can be advanced by respecting the need for open spaces. First of all, open spaces cannot fully play their roles if they are far away from the urban center. Of course, the edges of urbanization should not move too far away from the urban center. In the case of the Tokyo Region, for instance, the edge of urbanization has already reached areas about 50 km from the city center. This is obviously too far from the city center, and all efforts should be made against further extension outward. The urbanization of a city usually develops not in a round shape but in the shape of an open palm with transportation corridors such as railways and highways as its fingers. The second point is that farmlands and woodlands remaining between the fingers should be left as open spaces (the so-called green-wedge spaces) by all means. These green-wedge spaces have been left behind by urbanization because of inadequate transportation to them. However, these are more important than the open spaces located at the finger tips of urbanization, since they are closer to the densely populated areas and accessible to citizens on foot at a time of emergency even when the urban transportation network is disrupted. The third point is that even within the city areas, sizable open spaces—such as dry riverbeds and flood plains, which are necessary for flood prevention—should be kept from conversion into housing land. In addition, the woods on the slopes between alluvial and diluvial formations as well as the springs (often making ponds) and woods around them (in many cases, temples and shrines) are also open spaces that should be preserved by all means. However, farmlands left here and there in the middle of urbanized areas need no such exceptional classification as open spaces.

There should be no single farmland area exceeding 20 hectares in the UPA. The small farmland spaces within the UPA in principle cannot play the role of open spaces in the prescribed sense. A small vacant space of, for instance, several hectares would be unreliable as a refuge space at a time of town fire, if it is surrounded with wooden houses in congestion (a typical example of the case of a mass of people burnt to death at the backyard of the Honjo Logistic in the 1923 Kanto Great Earthquake). Therefore, conversion of such small farmland spaces into housing areas does not readily mean the loss of open spaces. Of course, there are among the farmlands in the urbanized areas those that can be recommended for use as town parks and children's playgrounds or as the spaces for public facilities such as schools and athletic field parks.

Housing Problem and Land Problem

This book has discussed the housing problem as it relates to the land problem and has emphasized that a solution to the land problem is the indispensable prerequisite to solving the housing problem. Then, you may wonder why the housing problem should be severed from the land problem. In the cases of rental houses, the land problem and the housing problem are obviously inseparable because land prices affect rents in one way or another, except for the case where a public organization purchases land and builds public housing, with rental users. A brief comment on the supply of public housing—the main purpose of this book is not the problems of public housing in general—will clarify how public housing supply affects the land price, and vice versa, in case a policy is implemented to positively increase the supply of public housing.

In Japan there are three categories of public housing—housing built by the Japan Housing Corporation, housing built by the local Housing Supply Corporations, and housing built by the local governments—all of which can be supplied at lower prices than private houses because of public subsidies. The housing land of these publicly built houses have generally been acquired at prices based on market price. The

Eminent Domain Law has seldom been invoked to provide land for the construction of public housing. (Ever since the inauguration of the Japan Housing Corporation in 1955, the law had been invoked for the corporation's land purchases only in six cases.) As a matter of general practice, the Japan Housing Corporation and local housing supply corporations have purchased lands from private dealers after the latter had arranged the required parcels. In response to informal requests by such public organizations, private dealers confidentially start advance purchases of the required plots so that they can sell these plots in a package to public organizations within the prescribed time. Therefore, it can be said that the public organizations' land purchase behaviors are virtually the same as the behaviors of private developers for acquisition of housing development sites.

Therefore, the development of public housing can be said to affect land prices when it stimulates demand for land.

In this aspect, the background of public housing land lots and lots with houses for direct sale to users must be described. Such public lots and lots with houses are usually priced cheaper than the private counterparts mainly because the capital costs of the Japan Housing Corporation and local housing supply corporations are lower. Such public housing corporations can not only expect fund appropriations, free of dividends, from the central government and local public entities but also are entitled annually to loans from the Ministry of Finance funds. Because their capital costs are cheaper, they can hold the purchased lands longer than the private developers, consequently supplying housing land lots and houses more cheaply than the market prices of the private counterparts in the neighborhood.

Since such public corporations can supply lots and houses at low prices, people reasonably prefer to purchase the public prepared lots and houses. Even those who have given up the hope for acquiring housing lots may well try to purchase the public prepared lots. A small number of fortunate people among them may be entitled by lottery to purchase the lots on sale, while the others may be less fortunate. After all, by supplying lots and houses, the Japan Housing Corporation and local housing supply corporations are merely taking over a segment of the expected buyers. It can rather be said that they are acting to increase demand for lots and houses by inciting aspirations for a possibility of acquiring houses among the people who might have already given up such aspirations if such cheaper priced public lots and houses were nonexistent. If the accommodating capacity of the Japan Housing Corporation and local housing supply corporations were physically larger than the private housing tracts, the story would have been different. However, in terms of same price level, the private tracts have larger accommodating capacity because the private developers sell housing land in smaller lots. The public lots and houses have no merit other than to offer by lottery special benefits to a fortunate minority at the cost of public funds. The fact that the new settlers in the public houses can soon sell their residences at higher prices than their acquisition prices clearly shows the futility of this system.

The rental apartment houses built by the Japan Housing Corporation and local housing supply corporations offer low rents. It is virtually impossible to find flats in any private housing building equivalent to those in public condominiums on the same rent level. The reason is simple. No private firm or person can profitably operate rental housing buildings under normal economic circumstances. Except for the case where farmers build rental houses in their own plots at the expense of public funds in suburban cities, there is no institutional system provided for landowners to attain large long-term loans at low interest rates. Therefore, they usually do not build medium- or high-rise housing that necessitates fixed capital in large amounts.

The rental flats in the public housing buildings can therefore be said to satisfy the low-income households who cannot be satisfied with the flats in the private-owned wooden apartment houses (especially with the limited floor spaces of such flats), while playing no role at all of taking over any segment of demand for the same categories of flats on the part of the private sector. Of course, the flats in this category in public housing buildings are playing a sensible role insofar as the private sector cannot supply quantitatively sufficient flats to meet the demand. However, as long as the users of such flats are in the income brackets below the appropriate level for the acquisition of houses, the public housing buildings cannot help repress the land prices, which are subject to demand among the households above a certain income level, no matter how many households are accommodated therein. On the contrary, as compared with rental houses and apartment houses built by landowners in their own plots, increasing public housing buildings tends to strengthen demand for land and duly accelerate the land price increases to the extent that the construction of such buildings is usually preceded by land purchases.

Finally, let us consider the low-rent housing built by the local governments. Regarding the rental houses built by the Japan Housing Corporation and local housing supply corporations, their rents are determined on the basis of cost with no direct subsidy though they can use funds at lower cost than the private counterparts. However, rental units built by local governments (hereafter called public rental houses) are classified into Class 1 public rent houses that have been built with their construction cost subsidized at 50 percent and Class 2 public rent houses with two thirds of their construction cost subsidized, and their rents are determined on the basis of construction cost minus the subsidies. Since these rents are lower compared with private rental houses and private apartments, they attract a large number of applicants. Though the criteria on the qualification for applicants at present includes an income limit, competition is still intense.

With this income limit taken into consideration, the public rental houses have even less effect than the rental housing buildings built by the Japan Housing Corporation and local housing supply corporations on decreasing demand for owner houses and thus have no effect on repressing land prices.

It should be noted that since a large part of the inhabitants in public rental houses are in relatively younger age groups and that life employment and the seniority wage structure prevail in Japan, they gradually become households that need houses as the number and age of their children increase. In this case, the cheaper rents may have accounted for increasing their ability to pay by allowing them to accumulate their surplus. In this sense, public rent houses can be said to increase demand for own houses as compared with the case where no such rental houses exist.

As already has been described, existing public housing in any form cannot repress land prices, even in cases where the supply of public housing increases as compared with the current level.

The role of such public housing is linked with social welfare policy to supply low-income households with rental houses. Therefore, no intention should be implied in this policy to repress land prices. What occurred, however, is that rising land prices have slowed down the construction of public rent houses, thus causing a delay in the planned advancement of social welfare. The housing problem is thus inseparable from the land problem.

Bibliography

Doebele, William, ed. *Land Readjustment: A Different Approach to Financing Urbanization.* Lexington, Mass.: D.C. Heath and Company, 1982.

Gamachi, Norio. *Fudosan Gyokai (Real Estate Businesses).* Tokyo: Kyoiku-sha, 1979.

George, Henry. *Progress and Poverty,* Vol. 1. New York: AMS Press Incorporated, 1973.

Hanayama, Yuzuru, and Kagato Shinzawa. *Chika to Tochi Seisaku (Land Price and Land Policy).* Tokyo: Iwanami Shoten, 1976.

Hanayama, Yuzuru. *Gendai no Tochi Shinwa (A Contemporary Myth of Land).* Tokyo: Asahi Shinbunsha, 1981.

———. "The Housing Land Shortage in Japan—A Myth." *Japanese Economic Study* 11 (1983): 3–47.

Hanayama, Yuzuru, and Tokunosuke Hasegawa. "The Land Market Structure on the Fringe of Tokyo." In Cullen, Matthew, and Sharon Woolery, *World Congress on Land Policy, 1980.* Lexington, Mass.: D.C. Heath and Company, 1982.

Hasegawa, Tokunosuke. "Shutoken Seibi Chitai ni Okeru Kukakuchi no Fuzon Jokyo" (Distribution of Vacant Lots in Suburbs of the National Capital Sphere). *Takuchi Kaihatsu (Housing Land Development)* 60: 3–15.

Hayakawa, Kazuo. *Jutaku Binbo Monogatari (A Tale of Housing Poverty).* Tokyo: Iwanami Shoten, 1979.

Horiuchi Kyoichi. *Toshi Keikaku to Yotokisei-sei (City Planning and Zoning).* Tokyo: Nishida-Shoten, 1978.

Jichi-sho (Ministry of Home Affairs). *Koteishisanzei Jokyo Shirabe (Annual Report on Real Estate Tax).* Tokyo: National Government Printing Office, 1968 to 1976 editions.

Jiyu-minshu-to Toshi Seisaku Chosakai (Urban Policy Committee, Liberal-Democratic Party, Japan). *Toshi Seisaku Taiko (A Program for Better Urban Policies).* Tokyo: Jiyu-minshu-to Shuppan-kyoku, 1968.

Keizai Kikaku-cho (Economic Planning Agency). *Kokumin Shotoku Keisan Nenpo*

(Annual Report on National Account). Tokyo: National Government Printing Office, 1970 to 1977 editions.

Kensetsu-sho (Ministry of Construction). *Takuchi Yoran (Housing Land Handbook).* Tokyo: Nihon Takuchi Kaihatsu Kyokai, 1977.

———. *Fudosan-gyo no Jittai (A Survey on Real Estate Dealers).* Tokyo: Ministry of Construction, internal report, 1979.

Kokudo-cho (National Land Agency). *Kokudo Riyo Hakusho (White Paper on National Land).* Tokyo: National Government Printing Office, 1973 to 1979 editions.

———. *Shigaikakuiki ni Okeru Nochi Riyo no Jittai (A Survey of Available Farmland for Utilization in the UPA)* Tokyo: National Land Agency, an internal report, 1977.

Kokumin Seikatsu Center (The Better Life Information Center). *Dai-toshi Shuhenbu ni Okeru Jutaku Shutoku (Acquisition of Houses in the Peripheries of Major Cities).* Tokyo: The Better Life Information Center, an internal report, 1978.

Minerbi, Luciano, et al. *Land Readjustment: The Japanese System.* University of Hawaii, Honolulu: Department of Urban and Regional Planning, 1984.

Nihon Fudosan Kenkyu-jo (Real Estate Research Institute of Japan). "Zenkoku Shigaichi Kakaku Shisu" (Annual Report on Urban Land Price Index). Tokyo: Real Estate Research Institute of Japan, annual edition.

Nihon Fudosan Kyokai (Real Estate Trade Association of Japan). *Shutoken Takuchi Kyokyu Jittai Chosa (Annual Report on Housing Land Supply in the National Capital Sphere).* Tokyo: Nihon Fudosan Kyokai, 1970 to 1978 editions.

Samuelson, Paul. *Economics,* 10th Ed. New York: McGraw-Hill Book Company, 1976.

Shibata, Tokue. *Nihon no Toshi Seisaku (Urban Policy in Japan).* Tokyo: Yuhi-kaku, 1978.

Sorifu Tokei-Kyoku (The Prime Minister's Office, Statistical Division). *Jutaku Tokei Chosa (Housing Survey—1978).* Tokyo: National Government Printing Office, 1980.

———. *Nihon no Jinko—1970 (National Census—1970).* Tokyo: National Government Printing Office, 1973.

Tanaka, Kakuei. *Nihon Retto Kaizo Ron (A Plan for Remodeling the Japanese Archipelago).* Tokyo: Nikkan Kogyo Shinbun-sha, 1972.

———. *Building A New Japan.* Tokyo: The Simul Press, Incorporated, 1972.

Tokyo Shi (Tokyo Municipal Government). *Teito Fukko Kukaku Seiri-shi (Record of Land Readjustment for the Reconstruction of the Imperial Capital City).* Tokyo: Tokyo Municipal Government, 1932.

Tokyo-to (Tokyo Metropolitan Government). *Tokyo-to no Jinko Ido no Jittai (The Present Situation of Population Movement in Tokyo Metropolis).* Tokyo: Tokyo Metropolitan Government, an internal report, 1979.

———. *Tokyo no Tochi Riyo (Annual Report on Land Use in the Tokyo Metropolitan Area).* Tokyo: Tokyo Metropolitan Government Printing Office, annual edition.

Tokyu Fudosan Kabushiki Kaisha (Tokyu Land Corporation). *Chika Bunpu-zu (Land Price Map)*. Tokyo: Tokyo Land Corporation, annual edition.

Toshi Kaihatsu Kyokai (Urban Development Association). *Minkan Takuchi Kaihatsu to Shakai Shihon Tohi (Private Housing Land Development and Social Capital Investment)*. Tokyo: Toshi Kaihatu Kyokai, 1977.

Index

About the Author

Yuzuru Hanayama is a professor of economics at Tokyo Institute of Technology. His many academic appointments include Visiting Fellow at Harvard University and Senior Fellow at the East-West Center. He received his Ph.D. in agricultural science in 1967 from the graduate school of the University of Tokyo. Professor Hanayama is a member of the Land and Housing Council of the Japanese Ministry of Construction and is a specialist member of the Pollution Council of the Agency for Environmental Protection. He has also served as a member of numerous Tokyo metropolitan boards and has contributed to many publications.